Panic Disorder

in the

Medical Setting

Panic Disorder

in the

Medical Setting

Wayne Katon, M.D.

Professor, Department of Psychiatry and Behavioral Sciences
University of Washington Medical School
Seattle, Washington

American Psychiatric Press, Inc.

Washington, DC
London, England

This publication was developed by the author under contract number 88-MO-304934-01D from the National Institute of Mental Health. Douglas B. Kamerow, M.D., M.P.H., and Ann A. Hohmann, Ph.D., M.P.H., served as the NIMH project officers.

The opinions expressed herein are the views of the author and do not necessarily reflect the official position of the National Institute of Mental Health or any other part of the U.S. Department of Health and Human Services.

This monograph was previously published as DHHS Publication No. (ADM)89-1629.

American Psychiatric Press, Inc.,
1400 K Street, N.W., Washington, DC 20005

Library of Congress Cataloging-in-Publication Data

Katon, Wayne.
     Panic Disorder in the medical setting/Wayne Katon.
     p.   cm.
     Reprint. Originally published in the series: DHHS publication;
no. (ADM) 89-1629.
     Includes bibliographical references.
     Includes index.
     ISBN 0-88048-372-5 (alk. paper)
     1. Panic disorders. 2. Panic disorders—Case studies. I. Title.
     [DNLM: 1. Fear. 2. Phobic Disorders—case studies. 3. Phobic
Disorders—diagnosis. 4. Phobic Disorders—therapy. WM 178 K195p 1989]
RC535.K38 1990
616.85′223—dc20
DNLM/DLC
for Library of Congress   90-875
                                                               CIP

British Cataloguing in Publication Data

A CIP record is available from the British Library.

Contents

Case Examples

Foreword

Panic disorder (with or without agoraphobia) is one of the most common — and, for patients, disabling—psychiatric disorders encountered in general medical settings. From a recent study in a primary care practice setting, investigators estimated that the 1-month prevalence of panic disorder among primary care patients is 1.4 percent (Von Korff et al. 1987). The estimate from the community-based Epidemiologic Catchment Area study is that in any month 0.5 percent of the population will have this diagnosis (Regier et al. 1988). Because a number of medical and mental disorders may mimic symptoms similar to panic disorder, an accurate differential diagnosis is essential — but often difficult.

During the past two decades, enormous strides have been made in elucidating the dysfunctional brain mechanisms underlying panic disorder, specifying empirically based diagnostic criteria, and developing effective treatments. All of these developments have given knowledgeable primary care physicians and psychiatric specialists alike newfound power to recognize and ameliorate the course of this once-daunting disorder. However, many practitioners, especially those trained before these developments occurred, may have had little opportunity to stay abreast of all these advances. Further, only a limited amount of the recent psychiatric research literature related to panic disorder has been translated into practical advice for primary care physicians.

This volume was written to fill that knowledge gap by providing busy primary care practitioners (and their mental health consultants) with practical, state-of-the-art diagnostic and treatment techniques for panic disorder. It is intended to aid clinicians in recognizing and treating patients with this common mental disorder and in identifying when psychiatric consultation or referral is required.

This volume includes up-to-date information on the natural course, clinical characteristics, epidemiology, psychobiology, and treatment of panic disorder. Dr. Katon cogently discusses the challenge of diagnosing panic disorder, the medical illnesses associated with it, and the bases for making a differential diagnosis. In addition, he suggests ways to provide followup care for these patients in primary care settings and offers guidelines for psychiatric referral. He has also thoughtfully included a list of articles and books related to panic disorder that should prove particularly useful for patients and physicians.

For the National Institute of Mental Health, which sponsored the development of this volume, it represents an important aspect of our research mission: closing the gap between the research laboratory and the clinician's office. Because primary care practitioners are the main source of ambulatory care for the mentally ill, we are particularly eager to asssure that clinically relevant results of mental health research reach such clinicians quickly, in a form they will find readily accessible and useful in day-to-day practice. I believe that these goals are admirably met in this volume.

Lewis L. Judd, M.D.
Director
National Insititute of Mental Health

Preface

The following case is presented to intrigue and interest the primary care physician and to demonstrate that panic disorder is associated with many common patient symptoms seen in clinics every day.

Mr. W was a 22-year-old graduate student who presented to his family physician with acute episodes of chest pain and shortness of breath. Mr. W had recently moved to a new city, where he had few friends or family, to begin graduate school. His physician performed a careful physical examination and electrocardiogram, which were both negative. Then he brought up the subject of stress and anxiety, and the patient readily agreed that both the recent relocation to a new city and graduate school were quite stressful. He was referred to psychotherapy in the student health service. Mr. W's symptoms continued, and over the next 2 years, he made about 20 visits to his primary care physician for various somatic symptoms. Laboratory tests and physical examinations were all negative. In his second year of graduate school, he developed acute episodes of epigastric distress that often awakened him from sleep and were relieved by antacids. During this time, the patient lost 20 pounds. An upper gastrointestinal series proved negative, and the patient refused endoscopy.

Finally, after 2 years of symptoms, the patient was referred for psychiatric consultation. He reported that his episodes of chest pain and shortness of breath were often accompanied by tachycardia, sweating, tremulousness, and a feeling that he was going to die. His epigastric distress frequently followed these acute episodes. Since the episodes began, he had become increasingly fearful of social situations, and he now avoided going to parties, to the theater, or to restaurants. The patient was diagnosed as meeting DSM-III criteria for panic disorder, and he was started on imipramine 25 mg at night, which was gradually increased to 100 mg over 2 weeks. His acute episodes of autonomic symptoms decreased over 3 to 4 weeks, and his avoidance of social situations gradually decreased over 3 months. Over the next 3 years, the patient only visited his family physician twice for yearly physical exams.

The above case emphasizes many points that are covered in this monograph:

- The association between panic disorder and stressful life events
- The frequent association between panic disorder and hypochondriacal complaints and high utilization of medical care
- The frequent misdiagnosis of panic disorder in primary care
- The association of panic disorder with psychophysiologic illness such as peptic ulcer disease
- The association of panic disorder with phobic behavior
- The rapid amelioration of panic disorder with specific psychopharmacologic and/or cognitive-behavioral treatment
- The decrease in hypochondriacal behavior and high medical utilization with effective treatment of panic disorder

Acknowledgments

This publication benefited from the critical review provided by the following experts in the mental health field: Donald F. Klein, M.D., New York State Psychiatric Institute; R. Bruce Lydiard, Ph.D., M.D., Department of Psychiatry and Behavioral Sciences, Medical University of South Carolina; David A. Katerndahl, M.D., Department of Family Practice, University of Texas; James T. Marron, M.D., Department of Family Practice, University of New York; Thomas W. Uhde, M.D., Division of Intramural Research, National Institute of Mental Health; David H. Barlow, Ph.D., Department of Psychology, State University of New York; and Jack D. Maser, Ph.D., Division of Clinical Research, National Institute of Mental Health. The Institute gratefully acknowledges their reviews and comments.

Introduction

Mental Illness in the Medical Setting

Data from epidemiologic and mental health services research suggest that 50 to 60 percent of patients with mental illness in the United States are treated exclusively within the general medical care system (Regier et al. 1978; Shapiro et al. 1984). These findings stimulated Regier and colleagues (1978) to label primary care medicine a major part of the "de facto" mental health service of the United States. Since more severe disorders such as schizophrenia, manic depressive illness, and the personality disorders are preferentially referred to the mental health system, an even higher percentage of patients with anxiety and depression are treated exclusively in the general health care system, especially in primary care. The recent National Institute of Mental Health (NIMH) Epidemiologic Catchment Area (ECA) study demonstrated that over a 6-month period, 70 percent of patients with affective illness visited a general medical care clinic whereas only 20 percent visited a mental health professional (Shapiro et al. 1984).

Epidemiologic studies have found that from 25 to 33 percent of primary care patients suffer from a mental disorder diagnosable on a structured psychiatric interview (Hoeper et al. 1979; Bridges and Goldberg 1985). Perhaps another 20 percent have transient stress-induced mental symptoms or chronic subclinical symptoms that do not meet research criteria, but are nonetheless associated with significant patient suffering and distress (Stoeckle et al. 1964).

Two decades of studies have demonstrated that, despite the high prevalence of mental illness in primary care patients, one-third to one-half of these psychiatric illnesses are not accurately diagnosed by their physicians (Nielson and Williams 1980; Schulberg et al. 1985; Katon 1987). Recent studies showed that somatization is the primary reason for this lack of diagnosis (Bridges and Goldberg 1985; Katon 1987). Somatization can be described as the presentation of psychosocial distress in an idiom of physical symptomatology and a coping style of increased health care utilization (Katon et al. 1984).

Mental illness is associated with amplification of chronic medical symptoms as well as psychophysiologic symptoms (headache, epigastric pain, insomnia). The tendency to amplify symptoms and the stigma of mental illness

1

are the primary reasons that many patients present with somatic complaints when suffering from a mental illness. Bridges and Goldberg (1985) demonstrated that 95 percent of patients with anxiety and depression were correctly diagnosed when they described their psychologic distress as their presenting complaint. However, 48 percent of the patients with mental illness who presented with somatic complaints or complaints about their chronic medical illnesses were misdiagnosed or not accurately perceived to have a mental disorder by their primary care physicians.

Several researchers have shown that a small percentage of patients consume a major portion of health care. Collyer (1979) found that 3.6 percent of his primary care clinic population used 10 percent of his contacts and one-third of his time over a 1-year period. Katon and colleagues (1990) found that 10 percent of enrollees in a large health maintenance organization used approximately one-third of all outpatient visits in an 18-month period, and that 20 percent used more than 50 percent of all outpatient visits. Furthermore, these patients were likely to sustain utilization well above normative levels. Prior research indicated that frequent users of health care are consistently found to have higher levels of psychologic distress, as well as poorer physical health status, than low utilizers (McFarland et al. 1985; Densen et al. 1959). Katon and colleagues (1990) demonstrated that almost half of screened high utilizers (patients in the top 10 percent of 18 primary care physician panels) were psychologically distressed. Moreover, 58 percent of these distressed high utilizers had either a current DSM-III anxiety disorder (panic disorder or generalized anxiety) or affective disorder (major depression or dysthymic disorder).

Two studies found that anxiety represented the fifth and fifteenth, respectively, most common medical or psychiatric diagnoses in primary care (Valbona 1973; Marsland et al. 1976). Moreover, the 1980-81 National Ambulatory Medical Care Survey, which gathered information on approximately 90,000 patient visits to a nationally representative sample of private physicians from nine medical specialty groups, determined that anxiety and nervousness accounted for 11 percent of all visits to physicians. Other physiologic complaints often associated with severe anxiety were also reported frequently, such as headache and dizziness (11.2 percent) and abdominal or stomach pain (7.5 percent) (Schurman et al. 1985).

Further evidence of the prevalence of anxiety in medical patients was provided by a recent survey of 350 primary care physicians who rated anxiety disorders as the most common psychiatric problem seen in their clinics (Orleans et al. 1985). Antianxiety medications in general, and benzodiazepines in particular, have consistently been among the most frequently prescribed medications in the United States over the last 15 years, and more than 80 percent of these prescriptions were written by primary care physicians (Hollister 1980). One study showed that 18 percent of more than 1,500 randomly selected primary care patients in 15 group practices were prescribed minor tranquilizers during a 6-month period (Wells et al. 1986). Not only is pathologic anxiety a primary reason for patients to visit physicians and a common etiology for psychophysiologic complaints, but it also represents a psychologic response to acute or chronic medical illness. Zung (1979) demonstrated that pathologic anxiety (defined as a score greater than 45 on the Zung Self-Rating Anxiety Scale) occurs in 9 percent of people in the community, 32 percent of patients seeking medical care from primary care physicians, and 52 percent of patients with a known cardiologic illness. Anxiety frequently causes patients to amplify complaints of organic illness and increase utilization of health care (Katon and Roy-Byrne 1989). For example, Dirks and colleagues (1980) found that patients with asthma and severe anxiety had three times as many hospitalizations as asthmatic patients with similar degrees of physiologic asthma, but low levels of anxiety.

Studies of primary care patients with mental illness have shown that these patients use about twice as much nonpsychiatric medical care as patients without mental illness (Hankin and Oktay 1979). Thus, patients with mental illness are overrepresented among patients who actually use clinical care over a 1-year period. This makes it essential for primary care physicians to start to accurately diagnose and treat or refer these patients appropriately, to decrease patient suffering as well as to decrease the stress on physicians of primary care practice.

Early accurate recognition and treatment of mental illness may decrease somatization and maladaptive illness behavior in these patients (Bridges and Goldberg 1985). Somatization frequently leads to high clinical utilization and potential harm to patients through inappropriate or invasive use of medical technology as well as to dependence on health care providers to meet psychosocial needs redefined as health care needs (Katon et al. 1984).

This monograph focuses on the diagnosis and treatment of panic disorder, a subtype of anxiety that frequently affects primary care patients but is often not accurately diagnosed. The philosophy underlying this work is that enhanced accuracy of diagnosis of patients with panic disorder will lead to more effective and appropriate care for these patients. This monograph reviews the latest epidemiologic, psychobiologic, and treatment studies on panic disorder and clarifies the relationship between panic disorder and other common psychiatric illnesses, somatic symptoms, and medical illnesses.

Chapter 1

Panic Disorder: Three Stages of Development

Panic disorder is a subtype of anxiety manifested by discrete periods of apprehension or fear and at least four specific somatic symptoms (see Exhibit 1). To meet DSM-III-R criteria (APA 1987), at least some of these attacks must be spontaneous and appear unexpectedly when the patient is not exposed to a phobic stimulus or in a situation in which the person is the focus of others' attention. At least four of these anxiety attacks must occur within a 4-week period, or one or more of the attacks must be followed by a period of at least a month of persistent fear of having another attack.

Although patients subjectively feel short of breath or as if they are smothering, often they are actually hyperventilating. In fact, carbon dioxide, bicarbonate, and phosphorous levels have all been found to be lower in patients with panic attacks than in controls (Gorman et al. 1988a). This evidence suggests chronic hyperventilation, for although carbon dioxide levels change rapidly, changes in bicarbonate take longer to develop and are likely to be secondary to renal compensation for respiratory alkalosis (Stanburg and Thompson 1952). This may be a key factor in the chronicity and ready provocation of symptoms associated with hyperventilation and anxiety attacks in these individuals. Chronic hypocapneia may cause symptoms to be present much of the time, and minimal reductions of an already lowered pCO_2 may precipitate acute symptoms (Magarian 1982).

Patients with evidence of chronic hyperventilation often can be diagnosed by their occasional sighing or deep respirations during the medical interview. Respiratory physiologists have determined that just an occasional sigh or deep respiration is enough to maintain hypocapneic respiratory alkalosis (Magarian 1982). Signs and symptoms of hyperventilation disappear with effective pharmacologic or behavioral treatment of panic disorder. In most cases, hyperventilation is probably not the cause of panic disorder but simply an epiphenomenon of this severe anxiety disorder.

Chronologically, panic disorder develops in three separate stages, with patients potentially stopping at any stage or progressing through all three (Exhibit 2). Patients will often have their first attack or cluster of attacks after

Exhibit 1.   Diagnostic criteria for panic disorder

A. At some time during the disturbance, one or more panic attacks (discrete periods of intense fear or discomfort) have occurred that were (1) unexpected, i.e., did not occur immediately before or on exposure to a situation that almost always caused anxiety and (2) not triggered by situations in which the person was the focus of others' attention.

B. Either four attacks, as defined in criterion A, have occurred within a 4-week period, or one or more attacks have been followed by a period of at least a month of persistent fear of having another attack.

C. At least four[1] of the following symptoms developed during at least one of the attacks:

    1. shortness of breath (dyspnea) or smothering sensations
    2. dizziness, unsteady feelings, or faintness
    3. palpitations or accelerated heart rate (tachycardia)
    4. trembling or shaking
    5. sweating
    6. choking
    7. nausea or abdominal distress
    8. depersonalization or derealization[2]
    9. numbness or tingling sensations (paresthesias)
    10. flushes (hot flashes) or chills
    11. chest pain or discomfort
    12. fear of dying
    13. fear of going crazy or of doing something uncontrolled

D. During at least some of the attacks, at least four of the C symptoms developed suddenly and increased in intensity within 10 minutes of the beginning of the first C symptom noticed in the attack.

E. It cannot be established that an organic factor initiated and maintained the disturbance, e.g., amphetamine or caffeine intoxication, hyperthyroidism.[3]

[1] Attacks involving four or more symptoms are panic attacks; attacks involving fewer than four symptoms are limited symptom attacks.

[2] Depersonalization is manifested by a feeling of detachment from and being an outside observer of one's body or mental processes, or of feeling like an automaton or as if in a dream. Derealization is evidenced by a strange alteration in the perception of one's surroundings so that a sense of the reality of the external world is lost. Alteration in the size or shape of objects in the external world is commonly perceived.

[3] Mitral valve prolapse may be an associated condition, but does not preclude a diagnosis of panic disorder.

Source: Reprinted with permission from the *Diagnostic and Statistical Manual of Mental Disorders. Third Edition, Revised.* Copyright 1987 American Psychiatric Association, p. 237-238.

Exhibit 2. Three stages in development of panic disorder

| Initial acute panic attack or cluster of attacks | $\longrightarrow$ | Panic attacks increase in frequency
Phobias develop
Anticipatory anxiety and avoidance behaviors develop
Medical care seeking dramatically increases for somatic compliants | $\longrightarrow$ | Agoraphobia
Dependency
Dramatic changes in family system
Chronic somatization develops |

---

a variety of life stresses. Patients will usually describe this acute attack as extremely frightening and, at times, the worst experience of their lives. These first attacks typically occur suddenly and unexpectedly while the patients are performing everyday tasks (driving in a car, walking to work). Suddenly, they may experience rapid heartbeat, dyspnea, dizziness, chest pain, nausea or abdominal distress, numbness or tingling of hands and feet, depersonalization or derealization, trembling or shaking, sweating, choking, or a feeling that they are going to die, go crazy, or do something uncontrolled.

Primary care physicians may see patients after their first few attacks. The presenting symptom of these patients is often the single most frightening autonomic sensation, such as chest pain or dizziness, and they are convinced that something is dreadfully wrong with their body.

Not all patients go on to develop chronic symptoms of panic disorder (Katon et al. 1987a). A subgroup of patients will develop one or more attacks under stress, but with reassurance and education about the nature of their attacks and supportive therapy by their primary care physician will not develop incapacitating panic disorder. Many people may experience occasional attacks, but the diagnosis of panic disorder is reserved for those whose attacks occur with some regularity and frequency or where strong anticipatory anxiety develops after a small number of attacks (Hollander et al. 1988).

Norton and colleagues (1985) found that 34 percent of college students had suffered infrequent panic attacks, but only 2.2 percent met DSM-III criteria for panic disorder. Another study (Katon et al. 1987a) found that while 20 percent of primary care patients had met criteria for panic disorder at some time in their lives, another 18.4 percent had infrequent attacks and never met criteria for panic disorder. The patients with infrequent attacks had significantly higher scores on measures of anxiety and depression compared to controls. They may represent a population at high risk for the development of panic disorder and major depression when stressful life events occur (Brown et al. 1986).

Many patients move quickly to the second stage in which the anxiety attacks become increasingly frequent and severe and the patient develops anticipatory anxiety—fear of having a panic attack. During this second phase, events and circumstances associated with the attacks may be selectively avoided, leading to phobic behaviors. For example, a man who has an anxiety attack on a bus may become quite anxious the next time he has to take a bus (anticipatory anxiety) and may begin avoiding public transportation (bus phobia). In this phase, patients' lives may become progressively constricted so that they avoid even activities and places in which they previously felt quite comfortable.

In a prevalence study of panic disorder in primary care, patients with panic disorder averaged 4.8 phobias compared to 1.2 phobias in controls who had never experienced a panic attack (Katon et al. 1986). The patients with panic attacks tended to have multiple social phobias (fear of eating in public, crowds, speaking to a small group of people, speaking to strangers) as well as fear of situations where they feel trapped (elevators, public transportation, driving on bridges or freeways). Katon and colleagues (1986) also found that not all patients with panic disorder developed avoidance behavior and phobias after developing panic attacks, although almost all reported increased social anxiety subsequent to the development of panic disorder.

Vitaliano et al. (1987) studied patients' coping patterns in dealing with stress by a standardized coping questionnaire, The Ways of Coping Checklist (Vitaliano et al. 1985). This questionnaire evaluates the patient's tendency to use several coping mechanisms including Problem-Focused Coping, Wishful Thinking, Avoidance, Seeks Social Support, and Blames Self. The study determined that the way patients with panic disorder characteristically coped with stressful life events was a better predictor of whether the patient developed multiple phobias than the severity of their anxiety and depression (Vitaliano et al. 1987). This suggests that personality variables such as coping are intimately associated with the level of social disability the patient develops secondary to panic attacks.

During this second stage of panic disorder, patients often dramatically increase their use of health services, going from physician to physician with one or more frightening somatic complaints (Katon 1984). They frequently become quite hypochondriacal and focus on their bodies with anxiety and fear that they have a life-threatening medical illness. The types of symptoms they present with can be cues to the physician that the patient may have panic disorder. These are reviewed in the chapter on somatization. Accurate diagnosis and treatment are quite important in this second stage, for patients may develop multiple phobias and anticipatory anxiety that can cripple their social and vocational lives.

Overlapping with the second stage of limited phobic avoidance, a third stage may develop in which the patient acquires more extensive avoidance behavior and becomes agoraphobic. "Agora" means marketplace in Greek and agoraphobia literally means fear of the marketplace. In DSM-III-R (APA 1987), agoraphobia refers to a fear of being in places or situations from which escape might be difficult or embarrassing or help might be unavailable in the event of a panic attack.

The DSM-III-R criteria for panic disorder with agoraphobia cover stages two and three of panic disorder (see Exhibit 3). Thus, DSM-III-R lists the current severity of agoraphobia in stages between mild and severe, recognizing that some patients have only mild avoidance while others become homebound or unable to leave the house unaccompanied by a significant other.

Primary care physicians should ask whether the patient has begun to avoid any situations, especially social situations, since the attacks began. If the patient answers no to this question, specific inquiries about fear of crowds, public transportation, closed-in spaces (elevators, movie theaters, church), driving alone, and going out socially with friends are important diagnostic questions. It is essential to inquire whether the patient has become fearful of entering these situations *alone*, since many agoraphobic patients will enter fearful situations when accompanied by a spouse or significant other. One useful question is "Since these episodes or attacks started, if you went to a crowded movie theater alone (if they never go to movies, ask about church) and every seat was taken but you had a choice of any seat, where would you sit?" About 80 percent of the time, the patient will state "An aisle seat in the last row or near an exit." This question reflects the tendency for the patient with panic disorder to become afraid of being in places or situations where escape might be difficult or highly embarrassing in the event of a panic attack.

As the agoraphobia worsens (third stage of panic disorder), patients become increasingly dependent on their spouses, demanding that they accompany them when they have to leave home or enter social situations. Dramatic changes may occur in the family system, with both the spouse and children affected adversely by the patient's dependency, avoidance of social situations, and clingy behavior. The spouse and children may be forced to take over many of the patient's responsibilities, such as shopping, earning wages, and attending school meetings. The patient's vocation may be adversely affected by absenteeism and avoidance of social situations at work, e.g., business lunches, making new client contacts, giving oral presentations.

In this third stage of panic disorder, patients frequently visit their physicians regularly and are often reassured "it's just your nerves" or "stress is causing your symptoms." Thompson and colleagues (1988) have shown that agoraphobia is the most common phobia leading to use of health services, especially when it is accompanied by panic attacks. Several studies have demonstrated that most patients view fear and anxiety as late symptoms of

Exhibit 3. Diagnostic criteria for panic disorder with agoraphobia

A. Meets the criteria for panic disorder.

B. Agoraphobia: Fear of being in places or situations from which escape might be difficult (or embarrassing) or in which help might not be available in the event of a panic attack. (Include cases in which persistent avoidance behavior originated during an active phase of panic disorder, even if the person does not attribute the avoidance behavior to fear of having a panic attack.) As a result of this fear, the person either restricts travel or needs a companion when away from home, or else endures agoraphobic situations despite this anxiety. Common agoraphobic situations include being outside the home alone, being in a crowd or standing in a line, being on a bridge, and traveling in a bus, train, or car.

Specify current severity of agoraphobic avoidance:

Mild: Some avoidance (or endurance with distress), but relatively normal lifestyle, e.g., travels unaccompanied when necessary, such as to work or to shop; otherwise avoids traveling alone.

Moderate: Avoidance results in constricted lifestyle, e.g., the person is able to leave the house alone, but not to go more than a few miles unaccompanied.

Severe: Avoidance results in being nearly or completely housebound or unable to leave the house unaccompanied.

In partial remission: No current agoraphobic avoidance, but some agoraphobic avoidance during the past 6 months.

In full remission: No current agoraphobic avoidance and none during the past 6 months.

Specify current severity of panic attacks:

Mild: During the past month, either all attacks have been limited symptom attacks (i.e., fewer than four symptoms), or there has been no more than one panic attack.

Moderate: During the past month, attacks have been intermediate between "Mild" and "Severe."

Severe: During the past month, there have been at least eight panic attacks.

In partial remission: The condition has been intermediate between "In full remission" and "Mild."

In full remission: During the past 6 months, there has been no panic or limited symptom attack.

Source: Reprinted with permission from the *Diagnostic and Statistical Manual of Mental Disorders. Third Edition, Revised.* Copyright 1987 American Psychiatric Association, p. 238-239.

panic attacks that result from the frightening autonomic symptoms (Katerndahl 1988; Ley 1985). Thus, many patients view their symptoms of nervousness and anxiety as appropriate responses to severe physiologic sensations. These patients are especially likely to present with concern about one or more autonomic symptoms associated with panic disorder, such as tachycardia, chest pain, or dyspnea, and to answer physician queries about nervousness or anxiety with statements such as "Anyone with the physical symptoms I'm having (chest pain, dyspnea, dizziness) would be frightened" (Katon 1988).

During a study on the prevalence of panic disorder in primary care, Katon et al. (1987a) found that a positive response to the one screening question in the structured psychiatric interview—"Have you ever had a spell or attack when all of a sudden you felt frightened, anxious, or very uneasy in situations when most people would not be afraid?"—often did not accurately identify a substantial subset of patients with panic disorder. These patients were accurately identified by adding several somatic questions, the most sensitive being "Do you ever have sudden episodes of rapid heartbeat or palpitations?" The patients accurately screened by the somatic questions perceived that their anxiety was appropriate to the severity of their somatic symptoms. The patients identified by the somatic screening questions had significantly higher scores on measures of anxiety, depression, and somatization than did control patients without panic disorder.

Primary care physicians frequently see patients with panic disorder at an early stage in their illness. Accurate diagnosis and appropriate treatment at this stage can decrease hypochondriasis and high medical utilization as well as prevent disruption of vocational and social roles.

Chapter 2

Historical Background

The history of panic disorder in modern medicine[1] demonstrates the difficulty physicians have had for 150 years in separating panic disorder from cardiologic, neurologic, and other medical syndromes. The combination of psychologic and severe physiologic symptoms of panic disorder continues to befuddle physicians' diagnostic accuracy to this day.

The term panic is derived from Pan, the name of the dwarfish Greek god of nature (D'Aulaire and D'Aulaire 1962). Pan was a lonely and moody god. When he was sad, he went off by himself and hid in a cool cave. If a wanderer happened to come upon him and disturb him, he would let out a scream so terrifying that whoever heard it took to his heels and fled in a fear that was called "panic." Early descriptions of panic attacks were provided in the English literature by Thomas Burton (1924) in his 17th century classic text *The Anatomy of Melancholy*:

> Many lamentable effects this fear causeth in men, as to be red, pale, tremble, sweat, it makes sudden cold and heat to come over all the body, palpitation of the heart, syncope, etc. It amazeth many men that are to speak or show themselves in public assemblies, or before some great personages . . .

Physicians first began to describe patients with panic disorder in the mid-19th century. Many of these early descriptions were of patients with palpitations and chest pain who were referred to cardiologists. With no modern diagnostic tests (treadmill, angiogram), shorter lifespans of the general population, and four of the main symptoms of panic disorder (chest pain or tightness, tachycardia, dyspnea, and a choking or smothering sensation) being cardiorespiratory symptoms, it was difficult for these early physicians to discriminate patients with organic heart disease from patients with panic disorder. Indeed, Leff (1981), a cross-cultural psychiatrist, pointed out that the words angina, anxiety, and anguish are all derived from the same Greek root, which literally means to press tightly or strangle. Leff suggested that a single

---

[1] The development of this chapter was aided by an excellent historical article by Skerrit (1983) on anxiety and the heart.

term, angh, was used in early Indo-European tests to describe the sensation of tightness or pressure on the chest, and that differentiation of this term to connote separate emotional and somatic causes of similar sensations only came in the late stage of development of Western society.

One of the earliest descriptions of patients with panic disorder was written by Hope, a British cardiologist. In 1832, he described patients with nervous palpitations in one of the first English textbooks of cardiology:

> There are few affectations which excite more alarm and anxiety in the mind of the patient than this. He fancies himself doomed to become a martyr to organic disease of the heart, of the horrors of which he has an exaggerated idea; it is the more difficult to divest him of this impression because the nervous state which gives rise to his complaint imparts a fanciful gloom and desponding tone to his imagination.

A few years later, Williams (1836), another English physician, described patients with nervous and sympathetic palpitations of the heart.

Military Historical Reports

In 1871, DaCosta, a civil war physician, described a syndrome that he labeled "irritable heart disease" that included symptoms of palpitations, tachycardia, dizziness, shortness of breath, chest pain, gastrointestinal distress, and "nervous symptoms" (headache, giddiness, and insomnia). DaCosta, in a description that echoes modern-day theory, noted it was "most likely that the heart became irritable from its over-action and frequent excitement and that a disorder of innervation keeps it so." He theorized that both battle trauma and severe physical illness frequently precipitated the syndrome. After DaCosta's classic description, other wartime physicians described similar conditions in young male soldiers every decade or two.

In 1870, Myers, a surgeon in the Coldstream guards, described a syndrome similar to DaCosta's and labeled it "soldier's heart." During World War I, the subject of soldier's heart became quite popular; 39 papers were published about it in the 1916 *British Medical Journal* (Skerrit 1983). A new term, "effort syndrome," was introduced in 1917 by Sir Thomas Lewis. He described symptoms of breathlessness, chest pain, giddiness, exhaustion, palpitations, headache, sweatiness, shakiness, flushing, irritability, and cold extremities. With the United States entering World War I, the term "neurocirculatory asthenia" was introduced by Oppenheimer and colleagues in 1918. MacKenzie (1920) later suggested that these heart abnormalities were but a feature of a general condition later suggested to be a "war neurosis."

In 1918, the first provocative research was attempted to study the sympathetic nervous system role in effort syndrome. Fraser and Wilson injected adrenaline and felt they had reproduced these patients' symptoms. However,

Wood emphasized in 1941 that injections of epinephrine caused equal symptoms in controls and patients.

Culpin (1920) was one of the first physicians to emphasize the association of effort syndrome with anxiety and phobias and to point out that treatment should be aimed at the underlying nervous problem, not the heart. During World War II, Wood (1941) published an account of 200 cases seen in the first year of the war with major symptoms described as breathlessness, fatigue, nervousness, dizziness, left chest pain, palpitations, headaches, trembling, sighs, and flushes. He concluded that the syndrome was due to an association between effort and fear, and favored psychotherapy as the treatment of choice. Jones and Lewis in 1941 also described the psychiatric conditions associated with effort syndrome, with anxiety the most common condition (31 percent of cases). The use of the term effort syndrome gradually declined during World War II and more specific psychiatric diagnoses came into favor (Skerrit 1983). Finally, Jones and Melleresh (1946), laying the foundation for future studies of lactate's association with panic disorder, found that effort syndrome sufferers would stop exercising at lower blood levels of lactate than controls. This was interpreted as a fear of damaging their hearts or "effort phobia."

Since World War II, several cardiologists have published papers supporting the "irritable heart" concept with new terminology such as "hyperkinetic heart syndrome" (Gorlin 1962) or "hyperdynamic beta-adrenergic circulatory state" (Frohlich et al. 1966). In the 1950s and 1960s, the term posttraumatic stress disorder (PTSD) came into favor to describe a psychologic state in young soldiers that resulted from massive trauma. Certainly, PTSD connotes a psychologic condition, but increased central noradrenergic activity has been postulated as a cause, and high levels of peripheral catecholamines have been reported (Kosten et al. 1987). The connection between PTSD and panic disorder is discussed in Chapter 6.

Nonmilitary Historical Reports

Beard in 1880 popularized the term "neurasthenia" for a cluster of illnesses long recognized by medical professionals under such terms as "nervous prostration," "nervous disability," and "nervous asthenia." Among its many symptoms were headache, a variety of kinds of pain, lack of concentration, noises in the ears, pressure and heaviness in the head, morbid fears including specific phobias (fear of disease and work), dizziness, palpitations, insomnia, dyspepsia, sweating, tremors, poor appetite, and exhaustion.

Sigmund Freud (1894) dissected out from neurasthenia a syndrome with a smaller group of symptoms, including free-floating anxiety or anxious expectation as well as anxiety attacks with symptoms of tachycardia, nervous dyspnea, sweating, tremor, diarrhea, dizziness or vertigo, paresthesia, and congestion. Freud also described the anxious expectation and anxiety attacks that often led to common physiologic danger phobias (fears of snakes, thunderstorms, darkness) and to agoraphobia. Although Freud emphasized that some patients would have attacks in which they focused on one symptom such as chest pain, dizziness, or tachycardia, his description did not mention prior accounts of irritable heart syndrome or soldier's heart. Freud initially theorized that sexual deprivation was the main cause of anxiety neurosis, but later progressed to the idea that psychoneuroses were caused by sexual and aggressive impulses going undischarged because they were repressed.

After World War I, Lewis (1940) recognized that the effort syndrome was also "one of the commonest chronic afflictions of sedentary town dwellers." Between the late 1920s and early 1940s, dyspnea associated with sighing respirations was noted by several clinicians as a common manifestation of chronic hyperventilation (Wolf 1947). In 1938, Soley and Schoch reported that all the symptoms of soldier's heart could be accounted for by involuntary hyperventilation and the resulting respiratory alkalosis. Also in the late 1930s, reports of "cardiac neurosis" began to appear in the literature. This was defined by Caughey (1939) as a neurosis in which circulatory manifestations are the main subjective and objective features of the clinical problem.

Skerrit (1983) pointed out that medical authors still tend to see anxiety neurosis (or panic disorder) from the viewpoint of symptoms presenting to their own specialty. Thus, cardiologists diagnose patients with mitral valve prolapse (MVP), labile hypertension, hyperdynamic beta-adrenergic state, and atypical chest pain without recognizing a common overlap with panic disorder. Pulmonary physicians similarly write about hyperventilation syndrome; gastroenterologists, irritable bowel syndrome; and neurologists, patients with unexplained dizziness, without recognizing that these symptoms are often part of a larger syndrome—panic disorder.

A historical review would be incomplete without mention of two seminal psychopharmacologic breakthroughs in the treatment of panic disorder in England and the United States. In the early 1960s in England, Roth (1960) described the phobic-anxiety depersonalization syndrome and Sargant (1962) reported the effectiveness of monoamine oxidase inhibitors (MAOI) in patients with atypical depression (a subgroup of depressives who frequently had panic attacks). Meanwhile, in the United States, Donald Klein (1964) described the effectiveness of imipramine in treating chronically ill patients on a psychiatric ward who had symptoms of panic attacks and agoraphobia and had progressively constricted their activities until they were no longer able to travel alone for fear of being rendered suddenly helpless while isolated from family or friends. Klein found that treatment with imipramine decreased acute panic attacks and separation anxiety, and that the patients' agoraphobia gradually decreased as they were pushed to reenter feared social situations and found they were no longer subject to anxiety attacks. The striking aspect of Klein's study was that these patients had been nonresponsive to phenothiazines, sedative-hypnotics, and electroconvulsive therapy. Both Klein's and the English studies led to a biologic revolution in the field of panic disorder or anxiety neurosis, disorders that previously had been thought by many authorities to be primarily environmentally induced and thus treatable only with long-term psychotherapy.

Chapter 3

Epidemiology of Panic Disorder

Panic disorder occurs frequently in the general population. Four recent studies estimated that 1.6 to 2.9 percent of women and 0.4 to 1.7 percent of men have panic disorder (Crowe et al. 1983; Myers et al. 1984; Uhlenhuth et al. 1983; Weissman et al. 1978). These prevalence estimates are probably quite conservative because the panic disorder patient's tendency to somatize frequently leads to underdiagnosis (Katon et al. 1987a).

Several studies found that patients with panic disorder are overrepresented within the medical care system. Katon and colleagues (1986) randomly assessed 195 primary care patients, age 17 years and older, with a structured psychiatric interview, the NIMH Diagnostic Interview Schedule (DIS) (Robins et al. 1981). A total of 6.5 percent of patients met DSM-III criteria for panic disorder alone, and 6.5 percent met criteria for major depression and panic disorder. Finlay-Jones and Brown (1981) found, using a structured psychiatric interview, that 17 percent of 164 female primary care patients suffered from anxiety neurosis, with 8 percent suffering from anxiety neurosis alone and 9 percent having anxiety neurosis and major depression.

Two studies examined the prevalence of severe anxiety in primary care patients on self-rating scales of anxiety (Linn and Yager 1984; Zung 1986). These scales are quite sensitive to panic disorder, but not very specific; for example, cases of major depression, alcohol abuse, and generalized anxiety may also score high on these scales. These studies determined that 20 percent of 739 primary care patients (Zung 1986) and 12 percent of 95 internal medicine patients (Linn and Yager 1984) scored in the moderate to severe anxiety range on the self-rating scales.

Lower estimates of the prevalence of panic disorder were found by Von Korff and colleagues (1987) using the DIS (Robins et al. 1981) in a large, primary care epidemiologic study of predominantly middle-aged to geriatric-aged internal medicine patients; they determined that panic disorder occurred in 1.4 percent of patients.

In clinical samples, panic disorder is significantly more common in females than males, with a ratio between 2.5 and 3.0 to 1 (Sheehan 1983). However, in the NIMH Epidemiologic Catchment Area study of the prevalence of mental illness in several large U.S. cities, panic disorder was consistently more common in females, but only in one of the three large cities did the difference reach statistical significance (Robins et al. 1984). The predominance of females in clinical samples of patients with panic disorder may, in part, reflect the tendency of females to seek health care more frequently than males do. In clinical populations, the onset of panic disorder is generally between the ages of 17 and 30 years (mean age 22.5 years) (Sheehan et al. 1981). In the ECA study, the highest 6-month prevalence was in the 25 to 44 age group (Myers et al. 1984).

Panic disorder tends to be a relapsing, remitting illness. Wheeler and colleagues (1950) completed a 20-year followup of 171 patients diagnosed as having neurocirculatory asthenia. The criteria for neurocirculatory asthenia were roughly similar to the DSM-III criteria for panic disorder. Of the 171 patients, 73.3 percent had mild symptoms with no disability, 15 percent had moderate to severe symptoms, and 11.7 percent were well. Noyes and Clancy (1976) studied 57 patients with panic disorder and found that 16 percent were unimpaired, 51 percent were mildly impaired, and 32 percent were moderately to severely impaired at 5-year followup.

Followup studies of patients with agoraphobia have also been performed. Many agoraphobics' avoidance behavior decreases with time or behavioral treatment, but these patients frequently continue to have panic attacks. Roberts (1964) followed 41 agoraphobic housewives for periods of 1 to 16 years and found that 55.3 percent had improved, although virtually all the improved still had some residual symptoms. Emmelkamp and Kuipers (1979) reported that 75 percent of agoraphobics treated with behavioral therapy continued to do well at 4-year followup. Marks and Herst (1970), however, in a large sample of agoraphobic patients, found that only 20 percent reported periods of complete remission after their phobias began.

Overall, in the followup studies of patients with panic disorder and agoraphobia, approximately 50 to 70 percent of patients show some degree of improvement (Reich 1986). Total remissions are much less common, with some of the studies suggesting that 50 percent of patients have some disability and 70 percent are still symptomatic 20 years after the initial diagnosis.

In a recent study (Katon et al. 1987b), 25 primary care patients with past histories of panic attacks had significantly higher scores on psychologic tests of depression, anxiety, and phobic anxiety as well as significantly more phobias than 78 controls without any history of anxiety attacks. These data and studies suggest that untreated patients with panic disorder do improve without treatment; however, they are often left with residual symptoms such as avoidance behavior, multiple phobias, and higher psychologic distress, especially anxiety and depression.

Panic disorder frequently causes marked avoidance behavior and phobias; thus, it is important to review studies of patients after effective treatment in order to study and differentiate state and trait personality characteristics. Reich and Troughton (1988) found that approximately one-third of patients *who had recovered* from panic disorder met criteria for either a dependent, avoidant, or compulsive personality disorder. Avoidant personality disorder alone was present in about one-fifth of the patients with panic disorder. In clinical terms, patients with these personality characteristics are more socially insecure, easily hurt, and dependent on others in social situations. Tyrer and colleagues (1983) found that the presence of a personality disorder was the best predictor of chronicity of anxiety neurosis (the British term for panic disorder). Patients with a personality disorder and panic attacks are less likely to respond well to psychopharmacologic or behavioral treatments (Mavissakalian and Hamann 1987). Specific personality traits associated with poor treatment response include impulsivity, interpersonal sensitivity, subordination of one's own needs, and social and occupational ineffectiveness (Cowley and Roy-Byrne 1988). Intensive early psychiatric intervention may be especially important in patients with personality disorders who develop panic disorder.

Chapter 4

Etiology of Panic Disorder

Stressful Life Events

Klein (1981) hypothesized in early studies on panic disorder that anxiety attacks represent a discrete alarm system built into the biologic hardware of the brain that is often evoked when an individual is threatened with separation from a significant other; some patients are more prone to these attacks, owing to an acquired or genetic vulnerability. Gittelman and Klein (1985) were able to demonstrate that patients with panic disorder had higher rates of pathologic separation anxiety and school phobia as children than did controls.

Weissman and colleagues (1984) reported that panic disorder in the parents, in contrast to other anxiety disorders, conferred a greater than threefold increase in separation anxiety in the children. Rosenbaum and colleagues (1988) found that 90 percent of children of patients with agoraphobia (most of whom had panic disorder), compared with 10 percent of children of controls, had "behavioral inhibition," defined as the tendency to manifest excessive withdrawal, inhibition, and physiologic responses to novel stimuli and mild cognitive challenge. The authors suggested that these were genetic traits that could lead to agoraphobia depending on the environmental input in childhood. Moreover, separation anxiety and school phobia respond to the same psychopharmacologic agent that Klein demonstrated was effective in panic disorder—imipramine (Gittelman and Klein 1985).

Animal research has also supported Klein's hypothesis. Both infant dogs and rhesus monkeys respond with characteristic high-pitched distress, whines, and cries and apparent anxiety when separated from their mothers (Suomi 1984). Infant dogs and monkeys pretreated with imipramine did not emit these characteristic distress calls when separated from their mothers. This effect did not appear with any of several other pharmacologic agents.

In two recent uncontrolled studies, both Katon (1984) and Uhde and colleagues (1985a) reported significant separation events as frequent precipitants of panic disorder. Three controlled studies looked at stressful life events as precipitating factors in panic disorder. Finlay-Jones and Brown (1981) studied 164 young women attending a general practice clinic, using a structured psychiatric interview and a record of stressful life events. The raters of life events were blind to psychiatric diagnoses. Patients with anxiety neurosis, most of whom met DSM-III criteria for panic disorder, had a higher frequency of severe life events than controls, especially life events that connoted danger and threat. Patients with depression were more likely to report a severe loss, and patients suffering from both depression and anxiety neurosis reported both severe danger and severe loss before the onset of their psychiatric disorder. Roy-Byrne, Geraci, and Uhde (1986) found that, when compared to controls, patients with panic disorder had significantly more stressful life events and had a higher proportion of events viewed as extremely uncontrollable, undesirable, and causing severe lowering of self-esteem. In the only other controlled study, Faravelli (1985) determined that patients with panic disorder had more events involving the death or severe illness of a friend or relative compared to controls.

One caveat is that many primary care patients minimize or deny stressful life events (Katon 1988). These patients often selectively focus on the somatic manifestations of anxiety and do not like to see themselves as distressed or needy in any way. Interviewing a spouse or family member of this type of patient is often helpful and can provide additional important data.

The following case describes the development of panic disorder in the context of a threatened separation from a spouse. The case also demonstrates the tendency of patients with panic disorder to somatize and how the developmental trauma can add to a patient's vulnerability.

Panic Disorder Associated With Stressful Life Event

Mrs. S was a married physical therapist who presented to the primary care physician with complaints of dizziness, headaches, and paresthesias. She had had one hospitalization and two complete neurologic workups, both of which were negative, over a 3-month period. She had a normal CAT scan, electromyelogram, electroencephalogram, and lumbar puncture, and a neurologic examination revealed no lateralizing or abnormal findings. Despite these negative workups, Mrs. S was very fearful that these attacks were the harbingers of an impending stroke.

Further history revealed that she was the oldest of four children and that her father had died of a stroke when she was 14 years old. She had a poor relationship with her very critical, chronically depressed, distant mother, with whom she fought recurrently as an adolescent. Her mother accused her, at times, of causing her father's death by raising his blood pressure with her rebellious behavior.

Mrs. S revealed that she had been married for 6 months prior to the start of her symptoms, and that her relationship with her husband had deteriorated soon after the marriage began. She described her first attack as beginning after a verbal battle with her husband in which he stated angrily, "You are going to kill me, too" and left the house precipitously. She described later in therapy that this statement brought up painful memories of losing her father as well as the fear that her husband was going to leave her.

The patient described her attacks as not only including neurologic symptoms, such as headaches, dizziness, and paresthesias, but also tachycardia, shortness of breath, sweating, and a sense of impending doom. She had become increasingly fearful of going out alone since the attacks began, and she was much more dependent on her husband. The patient was diagnosed as meeting criteria for panic disorder and started on a daily dose of 25 mg of imipramine. This was increased to 100 mg over 10 days, with the resolution of her panic attacks over a 2-week period. The family physician and psychiatrist also worked with the patient with psychodynamic and marital therapy to help her stabilize her marriage and decrease many self-esteem vulnerabilities that she had had since childhood.

Genetics

Panic disorder is a familial disease. Several of the physicians who first described the syndrome recognized this familial tendency. Oppenheimer and Rothschild (1918) found a family history of nervousness in 45 percent of 100 World War I soldiers with DaCosta's syndrome. Wood (1941) described a family history of "probable cardiac neurosis" in a quarter of his World War II soldiers with the syndrome. In the first two systematic investigations, Cohen and colleagues (1951) found that 22 percent of first-degree relatives of patients with "neurocirculatory asthenia" suffered from the same disorder, and Noyes and colleagues (1978) noted an 18-percent morbidity risk for anxiety neurosis in first-degree relatives. The latter two studies both found females affected more frequently than males, with a ratio approaching 2:1, and found more alcoholism in the male relatives of anxiety neurotics than in control relatives. Although these studies suggest a high morbidity risk in first-degree relatives of patients with panic disorder, the data were collected by the family history method (i.e., the patients were interviewed about a history of mental illness in all first-degree relatives), which tends to produce a conservative estimate of morbidity (Andreasen et al. 1977). By directly examining first-degree relatives of panic disorder patients with a structured psychiatric interview, Crowe and colleagues (1983) found a 41-percent morbidity risk of panic disorder among first-degree relatives compared to 4 percent among controls. Consistent with the prior studies, an increased rate of alcoholism (15 versus 4 percent) was found among male relatives. The family history studies have all demonstrated a higher frequency of the disorder among first-degree relatives than would be expected, but these studies are not conclusive about the question of heredity (Torgerson 1983). The findings could be due to common environment as well as to common genetic vulnerability.

Twin studies offer an opportunity for resolving the question about the relative contribution of heredity and environment in the development of psychiatric disorders. Torgerson (1983) compared panic disorder rates in monozygotic (MZ) twins, who share the same genetic endowment, and dizygotic (DZ) twins, who are no more alike than the other siblings. Assuming that MZ and DZ twins are likely to have the same environment, then a finding of increased concordance for psychiatric illness in MZ compared to DZ twins is considered evidence for the importance of heredity in the development of the disorder. Torgerson found that 31 percent of MZ twins were concordant for panic disorder versus 0 percent of DZ twins, a highly significant finding. Overall, anxiety disorders with panic attacks were more than five times as frequent in MZ as in DZ twins.

Goldberg (1979) documented that 67 percent of patients with mental illness in primary care had mixed symptoms of anxiety and depression. Four studies of patients with panic disorder revealed that 50 to 88 percent of patients had a major depressive episode at some time in their lives (Breir et al. 1984; Cloninger et al. 1981; Raskin et al. 1982; Pariser et al. 1979). Taken from the opposite direction, 20 to 30 percent of patients identified as suffering from a major depression also have panic disorder (Leckman et al. 1983a). Thus, it is important to review the genetic studies of patients with panic disorder and major depression. Leckman and colleagues (1983b) found that major depression plus panic disorder in probands was associated with a marked increase in risk in relatives for a number of psychiatric disorders. Relatives were more than twice as likely to have major depression, panic disorder, phobia, and/or alcoholism than the relatives of probands with major depression without any anxiety disorder. Weissman and colleagues (1984) also found that having parents with major depression and panic disorder conferred more than a threefold risk of separation anxiety in the children. Childhood separation anxiety is believed by some authors to be a precursor of panic disorder in adulthood (Gittelman and Klein 1985). Others believe it is a childhood precursor of neurotic illness in general (Berg et al. 1974).

Developmental Antecedents

The finding that only 31 percent of monozygotic twins of patients with panic disorder also suffer from this severe form of anxiety suggests environmental influences in the development of panic disorder. Patients with panic disorder retrospectively recall more childhood fears and being more anxious as children than do controls (Cowley and Roy-Byrne, 1988). Raskin and colleagues (1982) found a higher rate of grossly disturbed childhood environments in patients with panic disorder than in controls with generalized anxiety. Uncontrolled studies have suggested that parental overprotectiveness (Solyom et al. 1976; Roth 1959; Bowlby 1973) and an excess of parental deprivation (Tucker 1956; Silove 1986) were more common in agoraphobic patients. However, recent controlled studies have found that agoraphobic patients recalled deficits in parental care and warmth during their early years, but only when they experienced, as a child, a sense of parental neglect and lack of care, either alone or with overprotection, did the risk of agoraphobia in adulthood appear to be increased (Silove 1986; Arrindel et al. 1983; Parker 1979). It is unclear whether the lack of parental care experienced by agoraphobic patients (most of whom also had panic disorder) is also experienced by patients with panic disorder who do not have agoraphobia. Joyce et al. (in press) addressed this question and found that patients with panic disorder and moderate to severe phobic avoidance were more likely to have grown up in a family with parental conflict, were more likely to have had symptoms of a childhood conduct disorder, and tended to leave school at a younger age than did patients with panic disorder and no or mild phobic problems. Taken together, the genetic, stressful life event, and developmental data suggest that panic disorder has both genetic and developmental antecedents and often begins in the context of stressful life events. Patients' developmental history, personality structure, and mechanisms of coping with stress are probably all important in determining whether an onset of panic attacks will lead to frequent and severe enough attacks to meet DSM-III-R criteria for panic disorder, as well as whether the patients will develop moderate to severe phobic behavior.

Chapter 5

Difficulty in Diagnosis—Somatization

Specific Somatic Complaints

The patient with panic disorder has cognitive, affective, and somatic symptoms (Table 1) and also suffers social consequences such as increased dependency on the spouse and vocational problems (Grant et al. 1983). In primary care, patients with panic disorder often selectively focus on and complain about the most frightening autonomic somatic symptom or on a psychophysiologic symptom caused by autonomic hyperactivity (e.g., diarrhea, epigastric pain, headache) (Katon 1984). Freud (1894) recognized the many modes of presentation of anxiety attacks and the frequent misperception by patients that they had a primary physical illness when he stated "the proportion in which somatic symptoms are mixed in anxiety attacks varies to a remarkable degree, and almost every accompanying symptom alone can constitute the attack just as well as anxiety itself." Panic disorder may also cause an exacerbation of symptoms from chronic medical illnesses such as asthma, angina pectoris, and diabetes (Katon and Roy-Byrne 1989).

In a study of 55 primary care patients with panic disorder referred for psychiatric consultation by their primary care physicians, Katon (1984) found that 89 percent of the patients had initially presented with one or two somatic complaints and that misdiagnosis often continued for months or years. The three most common complaints were of cardiac symptoms (chest pain, tachycardia, irregular heart beat), gastrointestinal symptoms (especially epigastric distress), and neurologic symptoms (headache, dizziness, vertigo, syncope, or paresthesias). Clancy and Noyes (1976) also provided evidence for somatization in panic disorder. They examined the medical clinic records of 71 patients with anxiety neurosis and found that 30 different categories of tests had been carried out. A total of 358 tests and procedures were performed on the group (range 0–11; mean=7.5 tests), and these patients had 135 specialty consultations. The most frequently requested tests were electrocardiograms (38 percent), electroencephalograms (24 percent), and upper gastrointestinal series (25 percent); the most commonly requested specialty consultations were from

Table 1.   Components of panic disorder

Cognitive	Affective	Somatic	Social
Worry	Anxiety or	Tachycardia	Dependency
Sense of foreboding	nervousness	Hyperventilation	Vocational
Sense of	Secondary	(patient	limitations
impending	depression	complains of	Isolation
doom or dread	Irritability	shortness of	
Exaggeration of		breath)	
innocuous		Tingling in hands	
situations as		and feet	
dangerous		Diaphoresis	
Exaggeration of		Dizziness or	
probability of		syncope	
harm in specific		Flushing	
situations		Muscle tension	
Tendency to be		Tremulousness	
inattentive,		Restlessness	
distractible		Chest tightness,	
Sense of unreality		pressure on	
Rumination		chest (pseudo-	
Loss of control		angina)	
		Headaches,	
		backaches,	
		muscle	
		spasms	

Source: Adapted from Grant et al. 1983, p. 909.

the cardiology, neurology, and gastroenterology services. These results document the frequency of cardiac, neurologic, and gastrointestinal symptoms in patients with panic disorder.

Lydiard and colleagues (1986) recently described a series of patients who had both irritable bowel syndrome (IBS) and panic disorder. IBS is a chronic gastrointestinal syndrome characterized by abdominal discomfort and pain with an alteration in bowel habits (cramping, diarrhea, constipation) in the absence of weight loss or demonstrable gastrointestinal pathology. Effective treatment of panic disorder also ameliorated the patients' irritable bowel complaints. Several patients with both irritable bowel syndrome and panic disorder were also described by Katon (1984).

Irritable bowel syndrome affects 8 to 17 percent of the general population (Drossman et al. 1982), and several studies have found that 70 to 90 percent of

IBS patients have diagnosable psychiatric problems, most commonly anxiety and depression (Young et al. 1976). Drossman and colleagues (1988) compared 73 IBS patients who received medical care for their symptoms to 82 persons with IBS who did not seek such care. The IBS patients visiting physicians had higher scores on psychologic tests of depression, anxiety, and somatization. The following case demonstrates the association of irritable bowel symptoms with panic disorder and the amelioration of both the anxiety and the irritable bowel syndrome with a tricyclic antidepressant.

The presentation of cardiac complaints by patients with panic disorder is especially likely to lead to expensive and potentially iatrogenic medical testing. Past studies have documented high anxiety and depression scores on psychologic tests of patients who had chest pain and normal coronary angiograms (Elias et al. 1982; Costa et al. 1985). Followup studies of these patients have consistently shown that the risk of subsequent myocardial infarction is low (Kemp et al. 1986), yet 50 to 75 percent have persistent complaints of chest pain and disability after normal coronary arteriograms (Ockene et al. 1980). These patients are frequently described in the medical literature as "cardiac neurotics" or "cardiac cripples" (Caughey 1939).

Three recent studies found that patients with chest pain who had negative

---

Panic Disorder Associated With Irritable Bowel Syndrome

Mrs. S is a 47-year-old teacher who presented to the primary care physician with left lower quadrant "crampy" pain and intermittent diarrhea and constipation. She had several prior gastrointestinal workups, resulting in negative upper and lower GI series and colonoscopy.

Mrs. S stated that her bowel tended to act up under stress and had been an intermittent problem to her throughout her life. She was referred to psychiatric consultation owing to her apparent nervousness.

Mrs. S gave a history of having suffered from five episodes of major depression. At the interview, she had depressed mood, but no other vegetative symptoms. She complained of episodes of rapid heart rate, shortness of breath, sweatiness, dizziness, and a sense of loss of control that often preceded her abdominal pain and diarrhea. Her family physician had treated her with an anticholinergic agent for her bowel symptoms without success.

The patient was diagnosed as having current panic attacks as well as a history of major depressive episodes. She was started on 25 mg of imipramine with the suggestion to increase by 25 mg increments every 5 days. On 50 mg of imipramine, her abdominal symptoms and panic attacks disappeared, and she remained asymptomatic over the succeeding year.

angiography or treadmill tests had a very high prevalence of panic disorder (Katon et al. 1988; Beitman et al. 1987; Bass and Wade 1984). Bass and Wade (1984) examined 99 patients with chest pain undergoing coronary arteriography. Forty-six had hemodynamically insignificant disease, and 53 had significant coronary stenosis. Twenty-eight (61 percent) of the patients with insignificant disease had psychiatric diagnoses compared to 23 percent of those with significant obstruction. The most common psychiatric diagnosis in the patients with insignificant disease was anxiety neurosis, and 52 percent of this patient group exhibited polyphobic behavior.

Katon and colleagues (1988) studied 74 patients with chest pain who were referred to coronary angiography. Using structured interviews, 43 percent of the 28 patients with chest pain and normal coronary arteries were found to have panic disorder compared to 5 percent of 46 patients with chest pain who had significant coronary artery stenosis. Patients with chest pain and normal coronary arteries had a significantly higher mean number of autonomic symptoms (tachycardia, dyspnea, dizziness) associated with their chest pain (5.2 versus 3.8, p < .05) and were significantly more likely to have atypical chest pain. Beitman and colleagues (1987) found that 43 (58 percent) of 74 patients with atypical or nonanginal chest pain and no evidence of coronary artery disease by electrocardiogram, treadmill, or angiography had panic disorder.

Ford (1987) reviewed the association between chest pain and psychiatric illness in the ECA study and found that 2.5 percent of patients complained of chest pain. Patients with chest pain were four times as likely to have panic disorder, three times as likely to have phobic disorder, and twice as likely to have major depression as controls without chest pain.

The above correlations documenting a high association between chest pain and panic disorder have more significant implications for the primary care physician than for the cardiologist. The cardiologist is more likely to be sent patients with multiple cardiac risk factors and to feel bound to refer them for cardiac testing. On the other hand, the most common primary care patient is a 20- to 40-year-old female, the subgroup with the highest prevalence rate for panic disorder (Myers et al. 1984) and a low frequency of coronary artery disease.

In all three of the above studies of patients with chest pain referred for cardiac testing, patients with negative workups were significantly younger and more likely to be female. Moreover, 40 percent of primary care patients with panic disorder present with chest pain (Katon 1984). Primary care physicians are the "filter" for cardiac referrals, and thus increased education about the association between chest pain and panic disorder may increase the accuracy of diagnosis and decrease unnecessary medical referrals and testing. The following case demonstrates the expensive and extensive testing that some patients with panic disorder receive.

Amplification of Somatic Symptoms

In primary care, three main types of somatization are seen (Rosen et al. 1982). The first and most common type occurs when patients present with somatic complaints after one or more stressful life events. Many of these somatic complaints are psychophysiologic in origin, such as headaches, epigastric distress, muscle spasms, and insomnia. They are probably secondary to the autonomic nervous system arousal associated with stress. The second type of

---

Panic Disorder Associated With Chest Pain and Other Somatic Complaints

Mr. D was a 35-year-old lawyer who presented to his primary care physician with acute episodes of chest pain, tachycardia, and labile hypertension. After these spells, he often had a sensation of stomach tightness and headaches. He was initially hospitalized in the CCU for 3 days where cardiac enzymes, EKG, echocardiogram, and exercise tolerance testing were all negative.

He was next referred to a gastroenterologist. Abdominal computed tomography (CT) scan, gastroscopy, serum amylase, and liver function tests revealed only a small duodenal ulcer. He was started on cimetidine with no improvement of his symptoms.

The patient was next referred to a neurologist. A CT head scan, EEG, EMG (for tingling in the hands), lumbar puncture, and neurologic examination were all negative.

The patient was then referred to an endocrinologist for the episodic labile hypertension. A workup for pheochromocytoma, carcinoid, hypoglycemia, and thyroid disease were all negative.

Finally, the patient was referred for psychiatric consultation because of his apparent nervousness and his wife's concern over his increasing depression. On psychiatric examination, he described the attacks of chest pain as not only accompanied by tachycardia but also by shortness of breath, tingling in hands and feet, diaphoresis, dizziness, and a sense of impending doom. In addition, he complained of depressed mood, insomnia, and decreased appetite, libido, and concentration. He was diagnosed as having panic disorder and major depression and started on imipramine, with a gradually increasing dosage to 300 mg daily at bedtime. He had a rapid recovery over a 1-month period with complete resolution of his symptoms. His labile hypertension resolved and his propranolol and cimetidine were tapered and discontinued over a 1-month period.

somatization is subacute and occurs when patients suffering from major depression and panic disorder selectively focus on the somatic components of these illnesses or on a psychophysiologic problem (headaches, dizziness, chest pain) precipitated by these illnesses.

The third and most difficult type of somatization to handle is chronic somatization. These patients frequently have chronic psychologic pain secondary to developmental insults such as being abandoned, physically and/or sexually abused, or severely neglected in their families of origin (Zoccolillo and Cloninger 1986; Walker et al. 1988). Their families were often chaotic, and alcohol and drug abuse were common (Woerner and Guze 1968). Drug and alcohol abuse have often been problems for these patients as well (Perley and Guze 1962). Frequently, this group of patients suffers from a sense of powerlessness in interpersonal relationships, and somatic symptoms become a mechanism for adapting to a threatening world. Somatic symptoms can be used to manipulate a spouse, avoid intimacy, and attain disability payments and prescription medications (opiates and benzodiazepines) (Katon et al. 1984).

Patients with chronic somatization may also suffer from panic disorder and/or major depression. The major developmental insults they have experienced should leave them prone to these affective problems. However, treatment of panic attacks or depression in this group of patients often leads to only 30- to 40-percent improvement in symptoms. Somatization often persists because of the benefits within the social support network that continue to reinforce illness behavior. Personality disorders are often associated with chronic somatization and, as reviewed above, personality disorders are a predictor of poor treatment response in patients with panic disorder.

It is important to emphasize that untreated patients with panic disorder frequently develop multiple complaints in multiple organ systems, and they can be misdiagnosed as suffering from chronic somatization or hypochondriasis, in general, or more specifically, somatization disorder (Katon 1986; Noyes et al. 1986). Pharmacologic studies of panic disorder have consistently demonstrated extremely high scores on psychologic measures of somatization (such as the somatization scale of the SCL-90) in patients with panic disorder and a reduction in their scores to normal levels with effective treatment (Sheehan et al. 1980; Noyes et al. 1986; Fava et al. 1988). Noyes and colleagues (1986) examined the hypochondriacal tendencies seen in patients with panic disorder. They found that, prior to treatment, patients with panic disorder scored as high on an index of hypochondriasis, the Illness Behavior Questionnaire (IBQ) (Pilowsky and Spence 1983), as did a group of hypochondriacal psychiatric patients. After treatment, patients with panic disorder had a significant reduction in somatic preoccupation, disease phobia, and disease conviction as measured by the IBQ. These data suggest that the majority of patients with panic disorder who present as hypochondriacs with a myriad of somatic symptoms can be effectively treated.

Katon (1984) studied 55 patients meeting DSM-III criteria for panic disorder who were referred to psychiatric consultation. Two-thirds of the female patients and one-third of the male patients had multiple positive symptoms on the medical review of symptoms and, as a result, spuriously met DSM-III criteria for somatization disorder (which require 14 or more medically unexplained somatic symptoms in females and 12 or more symptoms in males). In a later epidemiologic study of panic disorder in primary care using the DIS interview, Katon and colleagues (1986) determined that patients with panic disorder averaged 14.1 symptoms on a medical review of systems compared to 7.3 symptoms in a control group (p < .005).

The above studies indicated that panic disorder seems to lower the conscious threshold for worrying about physical symptoms—patients focus more on their bodies. Also, by the nature of autonomic nervous system arousal, panic disorder is apt to cause physical symptoms. Robinson and Granfield (1986) published a schematic model to help explain how emotional upset leads to the increased perception of somatic symptoms (Figure 1).

In this model, A represents a state of total comfort that rarely occurs physiologically. Diary studies of patients have shown that the average patient has a new symptom every 5 to 7 days, few of which are brought to the attention of a physician (Demers et al. 1980). Discomfort experiences that are subthreshold physiologic events stemming from internal organs, joints, muscles,

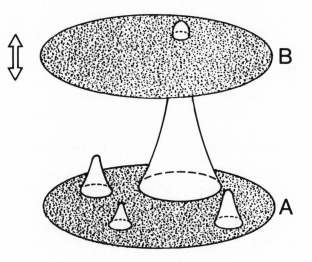

Figure 1. A model of symptoms. Source: Adapted from Robinson, J.O., and Granfield, A.J. The frequent consulter in primary medical care. *Journal of Psychosomatic Research* 30:587-600, 1986. Copyright 1986 by Pergamon Press. Reproduced with permission.

and so forth are represented by bumps on surface A. The height of the bump represents the seriousness of the experience in terms of its becoming consciously perceptible. During the emotional arousal of severe anxiety, surface A becomes increasingly bumpy, leading to psychophysiologic symptoms such as insomnia, headache, epigastric distress, and fatigue.

Surface B represents the threshold above which discomfort is consciously perceived. This surface is driven up or down by mood states, anxiety, stress, and focus of attention. Studies of patients with panic disorder or major depression suggest that these two illnesses tend to lower the B surface, leading to increased focusing, monitoring, and worrying about physical symptoms (Katon 1984; Katon et al. 1986; Katon and Von Korff 1990). The result of both the increased physiologic symptoms and bumpiness of the B axis and the increased focus and worry about these symptoms on the A axis is that the patient with an illness like panic disorder becomes anxious and obsessed by his symptoms and appears to the primary care physician to have hypochondriasis or somatization disorder. The danger is that the primary care physician, who sees many "trait" somatizers, will misperceive this as a trait or long-term irreversible part of the patient's personality. It is instead "state" somatization, which is subacute and directly resulting from panic disorder, and it is highly curable given accurate diagnosis and specific treatment.

The NIMH ECA study pointed to the difficulty that psychiatrists also have in distinguishing state or secondary somatization, resulting from an acute psychiatric illness such as panic disorder or major depression, from trait or primary somatization, a largely irreversible condition (Boyd et al. 1984). The data from this large psychiatric epidemiologic survey of five American cities demonstrated that patients who met DSM-III criteria for somatization disorder were 96 times more likely to also meet criteria for panic disorder than were patients who did not meet criteria for somatization disorder. Liskow and colleagues (1986) found that 41 percent of 78 female psychiatric outpatients with somatization disorder also met criteria for panic disorder. Similarly, Sheehan and Sheehan (1982) found that 71 percent of patients who met criteria for panic disorder also met criteria for somatization disorder.

One of the problems in differentiating these two illnesses is that symptoms such as chest pain, palpitations, shortness of breath, and dizziness are part of the DSM-III-R criteria (APA 1987) for both disorders (Exhibit 4). Also, one of the major criteria for the diagnosis of somatization disorder is an increased tendency to report physical symptoms that cannot be well explained medically. As mentioned above, research suggests that patients with panic disorder may report twice as many physical symptoms as do controls without psychiatric disorder.

How can the primary care physician proceed with diagnosis when faced with an obviously hypochondriacal patient with multiple unexplained physical symptoms? One differentiating factor is that somatization disorder usually

---

Exhibit 4.   Diagnostic criteria for somatization disorder

A. A history of many physical complaints or a belief that one is sickly, beginning before the age of 30 and persisting for several years.

B. At least 13 symptoms from the list below. To count a symptom as significant, the following criteria must be met:

1. no organic pathology or pathophysiologic mechanism (e.g., a physical disorder or the effects of injury, medication, drugs, or alcohol) to account for the symptom or, when there is related organic pathology, the complaint or resulting social or occupational impairment is grossly in excess of what would be expected from the physical findings
2. has not occurred only during a panic attack
3. has caused the person to take medicine (other than over-the-counter pain medication), see a doctor, or alter lifestyle

Symptom List:

Gastrointestinal symptoms:
1. vomiting (other than during pregnancy)*
2. abdominal pain (other than when menstruating)
3. nausea (other than motion sickness)
4. bloating (gassy)
6. intolerance of (gets sick from) several different foods

Pain symptoms:
7. pain in extremities*
8. back pain
9. joint pain
10. pain during urination
11. other pain (excluding headaches)

Cardiopulmonary symptoms:
12. shortness of breath when not exerting oneself*
13. palpitations
14. chest pain
15. dizziness

Conversion or pseudoneurologic symptoms:
16. amnesia*
17. difficulty swallowing*
18. loss of voice
19. deafness
20. double vision
21. blurred vision
22. blindness

Exhibit 4. (continued)

23. fainting or loss of consciousness
24. seizure or convulsion
25. trouble walking
26. paralysis or muscle weakness
27. urinary retention or difficulty urinating

Sexual symptoms from the major part of the person's life after opportunities for sexual activity:

28. burning sensation in sexual organs or rectum (other than during intercourse)*
29. sexual indifference
30. pain during intercourse
31. impotence

Female reproductive symptoms judged by the person to occur more frequently or severely than in most women:

32. painful menstruation
33. irregular menstrual periods
34. excessive menstrual bleeding
35. vomiting throughout pregnancy

* The starred items may be used to screen for the disorder. The presence of two or more of these items suggests a high likelihood of the disorder.

Source: Reprinted with permission from the *Diagnostic and Statistical Manual of Mental Disorders. Third Edition, Revised.* Copyright 1987 American Psychiatric Association, p. 263-264.

---

begins in the late teens and is chronic; the hypochondriacal preoccupation of these patients is only part of the generally chaotic lives these patients lead. The family histories of patients with somatization disorder often reveal a tendency for females in the family to have somatization disorder and the males to have antisocial personality disorders and/or be alcohol abusers (Woerner and Guze 1968). Developmentally, patients with somatization disorder usually were brought up in chaotic families where they experienced physical and/or sexual abuse, neglect, and abandonment (Zoccolillo and Cloninger 1986). Their adult relationships are often characterized by multiple marriages and relationships that are abusive (e.g., the spouse is an alcoholic who is frequently violent) (Guze 1976). In addition, patients with somatization disorder have a tendency to abuse prescription medications (opiates and general sedative-hypnotics), street drugs, and alcohol (Perley and Guze 1962).

    Even though the above characteristics often help distinguish patients with somatization disorder from those with panic disorder, accurate diagnoses are not always clear. Many patients with panic disorder are not accurately diagnosed and may go several years with their illness, often chronically somatizing. In a psychopharmacologic trial, Sheehan and colleagues (1980) found that patients with panic disorder had visited a mean of 10 prior physicians for their symptoms before an accurate diagnosis of panic disorder was made and specific treatment initiated.

When the etiology of chronic somatization is unclear, the following rationale should be used. Since somatization disorder is a chronic severe condition with no known specific treatment and panic disorder is highly treatable, patients with multiple unexplained somatic symptoms should be carefully screened for panic disorder (as well as major depression). If the patient meets DSM-III criteria for both somatization disorder and panic disorder, then the physician should err in favor of the diagnosis of panic disorder and a pharmacologic trial should be instituted.

Chapter 6

Differential Diagnosis of Panic Disorder and Other Psychiatric Illnesses

Affective Illness and Panic Disorder

Five studies have documented that 60 to 90 percent of patients with panic disorder develop a major depression at some time in their lives (Breier et al. 1984; Cloninger et al. 1981; Raskin et al. 1982; Pariser et al. 1979; Katon et al. 1986). Conversely, Leckman and colleagues (1983*b*) found that 21 percent of patients with major depression had a past or current episode of panic disorder. Data from the ECA project also revealed that people with major depression were 19 times more likely to have panic disorder and 15 times more likely to have agoraphobia than people without major depression (Boyd et al. 1984). Patients with panic disorder or agoraphobia and a history of major depression have been shown to have a more severe anxiety disorder, greater levels of past impairment, and a longer duration of panic disorder when compared to patients with panic disorder or agoraphobia and no history of depression (Breier et al. 1984). Leckman and colleagues (1983*b*) demonstrated that patients with major depression who also suffered from panic disorder had increased family prevalence of depression, anxiety disorders, and alcoholism.

Several studies have documented that major depression is not only a secondary complication of panic disorder, but frequently occurs autonomously (Breier et al. 1984; Katon et al. 1986). In one epidemiologic study of panic disorder in primary care, 44 percent of patients with panic disorder had an episode of major depression prior to their episode of panic disorder, 33 percent had an episode of panic disorder prior to an episode of major depression, and 22 percent had simultaneously occurring episodes (Katon et al. 1986).

Panic disorder and major depression clearly tend to occur in the same patient population, but it is not clear whether these two disorders have the same underlying etiology. Breier and colleagues (1984) offered two possible hypotheses: (1) anxiety and depressive symptoms are different phenotypic expressions of a shared genetic diathesis or (2) the presence of one disorder might lead to the development of a second disorder with a different pathophys-

41

iologic state (e.g., diabetes mellitus often leads to the development of coronary artery disease).

The data suggesting an overlap of panic disorder and major depression are supported by Goldberg's (1979) finding that 67 percent of patients with mental illness in primary care clinics had mixed symptoms of anxiety and depression. Thus, any primary care patient with symptoms of anxiety should be carefully screened for major depression and vice versa. The frequent co-occurrence of these disorders suggests that antidepressant medication (tricyclics or MAOIs) will be needed and that dosage levels used to treat depression should be employed. Specific psychotherapies (cognitive-behavioral) that increase the patient's confidence in coping with this severe anxiety disorder may also decrease panic attacks and secondary depressive symptoms (Rapee and Barlow 1988).

Alcohol Abuse and Panic Disorder

Research on panic disorder by Quitkin and colleagues (1972) demonstrated that patients with panic disorder often tended to self-medicate with sedative-hypnotic agents, especially alcohol and benzodiazepines. As panic disorder worsens, the patient frequently develops severe social phobias that interfere with social and vocational functioning. Also, the patient often develops generalized anxiety and not only suffers from the severe acute episodes of panic, but also from chronic symptoms of free-floating anxiety. Alcohol or sedative-hypnotics are sometimes used in desperation to try to control the anxiety. These agents usually have a short anxiolytic action, but the rapid drop in blood levels may then cause an exacerbation of severe anxiety and worsening panic attacks. Alcohol, in particular, may also worsen a psychophysiologic disorder, such as peptic ulcer disease or labile hypertension, that was precipitated by the panic disorder.

Alternatively, primary alcohol abuse and recurrent withdrawal may lead to a kindling effect on central controls of the sympathetic nervous system and the subsequent onset or worsening of panic disorder (Post et al. 1984). Kindling is the opposite of tolerance—with increasing exposure to a drug, the person experiences more intense effects rather than decreased effects. Thus, repetitive decreases in alcohol blood levels may increase the arousal and responsivity of the sympathetic nervous system. As seen in Exhibit 5, many of the symptoms of panic disorder and alcohol withdrawal are quite similar and, therefore, may present difficulty in differential diagnosis (George et al. 1988).

The ECA study determined that 13 percent of Americans met criteria for alcohol abuse at some time in their lives (Robins et al. 1984). Exhibit 6 lists the DSM-III-R criteria (APA 1987) for psychoactive substance dependence. The main feature of this disorder is that the person has impaired control of psychoactive substances (such as alcohol) and continues to use the substance despite adverse consequences to health, vocation, family, and social life. Some people never meet criteria for dependence on alcohol or other substances, but they have maladaptive patterns of use. These maladaptive patterns include recurrent use of alcohol when it is physically hazardous (when driving or using machinery) or continued use of alcohol despite recurrent social, vocational, or physical problems resulting from it. These types of maladaptive patterns without dependence are labeled psychoactive substance abuse.

For both females and males, the prevalence of drinking is highest and abstention is lowest in the 21- to 34-year age range. Alcohol abuse or dependence has three main patterns. The first consists of regular daily intake of large amounts; the second, of regular heavy drinking limited to weekends; and the third, of long periods of sobriety interspersed with binges of heavy daily drinking lasting for weeks or months (APA 1987). Alcohol abuse and dependence are often associated with abuse of other substances, including marijuana, cocaine, amphetamines, heroin, and sedative-hypnotics. The use of alcohol and these other substances together is most often seen in adolescents and adults under age 30. Although benzodiazepines are contraindicated in alcohol abuse, they are often prescribed by physicians in a misguided attempt to try to help stop or reduce the patient's craving for alcohol.

Exhibit 5. Overlap of symptoms of panic disorder and alcohol withdrawal

Panic disorder	Early alcohol withdrawal
Tachycardia	Tachycardia
Chest pain	Tremulousness
Dyspnea	Hypertension*
Sweating	Sweating
Hot and cold flashes	Diarrhea
Dizziness	Nightmares*
Tremulousness/shaking	Nausea, vomiting, or
Paresthesia	gastrointestinal distress
Faintness	Cramps
Nausea or	Exaggerated startle response
gastrointestinal distress	Fever*
Derealization or	Agitation, restlessness*
depersonalization	
Fear of loss of control, dying, or	
going crazy	

* Starred items either occur more commonly in alcohol withdrawal or only in alcohol withdrawal (nightmares, fever, and agitation).

Three recent studies of patients with alcohol abuse found that up to a third of them suffer from panic disorder, agoraphobia, or multiple social phobias (Mullaney and Tripett 1979; Bowen et al. 1984; Smail et al. 1984). Helzer and Pryzbeck (1988) have also shown that patients diagnosed as meeting criteria for alcohol abuse and/or dependence in the ECA study were more than twice as likely to suffer from panic disorder.

Smail and colleagues (1984) studied the co-occurrence of these disorders in depth to try to discern which problem occurred first and whether alcohol use ameliorated or worsened social phobias and panic attacks. They studied 60 alcohol abusers and found that 21 subjects had mild phobias and 11 had severe phobias. The more severely phobic males were also found to be the most alcohol dependent, and those with no phobias were least alcohol dependent. This effect was not found in females. All phobic alcoholics reported that

---

Exhibit 6. Diagnostic criteria for psychoactive substance dependence

A. At least three of the following:
1. substance often taken in larger amounts or over a longer period than the person intended
2. persistent desire or one or more unsuccessful efforts to cut down or control substance use
3. a great deal of time spent in activities necessary to get the substance (e.g., theft), taking the substance (e.g., chain smoking), or recovering from its effects
4. frequent intoxication or withdrawal symptoms when expected to fulfill major role obligations at work, school, or home, (e.g., does not go to work because hung over, goes to school or work "high," intoxicated while taking care of his or her children), or when substance use is physically hazardous (e.g., drives when intoxicated)
5. important social, occupational, or recreational activities given up or reduced because of substance use
6. continued substance use despite knowledge of having a persistent or recurrent social, psychological, or physical problem that is caused or exacerbated by the use of the substance (e.g., keeps using heroin despite family arguments about it, cocaine-induced depression, or having an ulcer made worse by drinking)
7. marked tolerance; need for markedly increased amounts of the substance (i.e., at least a 50-percent increase) in order to achieve intoxication or desired effect, or markedly diminished effect with continued use of the same amount

---

Exhibit 6. (continued)

Note: The following items may not apply to cannabis, hallucinogens, or phencyclidine (PCP):

    8. characteristic withdrawal symptoms

    9. substance often taken to relieve or avoid withdrawal symptoms

B. Some symptoms of the disturbance have persisted for at least 1 month, or have occurred repeatedly over a longer period of time.

Criteria for severity of psychoactive substance dependence:

Mild: Few, if any, symptoms in excess of those required to make the diagnosis, and the symptoms result in no more than mild impairment in occupational functioning or in usual social activities or relationships with others.

Moderate: Symptoms or functional impairment between "Mild" and "Severe."

Severe: Many symptoms in excess of those required to make the diagnosis, and the symptoms markedly interfere with occupational functioning or with usual social activities or relationships with others.

In partial remission: During the past 6 months, some use of the substance and some symptoms of dependence.

In full remission: During the past 6 months, either no use of the substance, or use of the substance and no symptoms of dependence.

Source: Reprinted with permission from the *Diagnostic and Statistical Manual of Mental Disorders. Third Edition, Revised.* Copyright 1987 American Psychiatric Association, p. 167-168.

---

alcohol had helped them cope in feared situations, and almost all had deliberately used it for this purpose.

In a subsequent study of 24 hospitalized alcohol abusers with panic disorder and multiple social phobias, periods of heavy drinking and dependence on alcohol were associated with an exacerbation of agoraphobia and social phobias (Stockwell et al. 1984). Subsequent periods of abstinence were associated with substantial improvements in these anxiety states. Thus, although alcohol was often used to try to cope with panic attacks and social phobias, it paradoxically made these anxiety disorders worse as alcohol abuse became more severe. The authors hypothesized that the worsening of phobias resulted from the repeated avoidance of fear through drinking and the increased anxiety from rapidly fluctuating blood levels of alcohol.

The implications of this research for the primary care physician is that all patients with panic disorder, agoraphobia, social phobias, and generalized anxiety should be carefully screened for alcohol and other psychoactive substance abuse. If alcohol abuse and/or other psychoactive substance abuse is

---

Panic Disorder and Secondary Alcohol Abuse

Mr. M was a 35-year-old laboratory technician who developed acute anxiety attacks with symptoms of tachycardia, shortness of breath, dizziness, sweating or diaphoresis, and a fear of impending death several weeks after his woman friend broke off their relationship. They had lived together for 3 years and had had recurrent relationship problems for the last year. Mr. M developed severe social phobias that prohibited participation in group meetings of his research group and eating in the hospital cafeteria. He began to drink the grain alcohol from his laboratory prior to research meetings to try to decrease his anxiety, soon escalating the dosage and also drinking wine at night to help with sleep. He presented to his family physician with hematemesis and melena approximately 3 months after the start of the panic attacks and 2 months after escalating his drinking. He was admitted to the inpatient service with a hematocrit of 20. He received several blood transfusions and was found on endoscopy to have had a large bleed from a gastric ulcer. He was quite tremulous, with increased pulse and blood pressure for 3 to 4 days, necessitating 25 mg of librium TID initially. He was seen in psychiatric consultation and diagnosed as having panic disorder and secondary alcohol abuse. He gave no past history of either psychiatric problem prior to the current episode. After 14 days of sobriety, Mr. M was still having frequent anxiety attacks and severe social anxiety. He was started on imipramine 25 mg with dosages increased to 100 mg over 10 days, made a rapid recovery, and was well on 2-year followup.

---

present, that disorder should be treated first and the patient reassessed after detoxification and alcohol treatment. If panic attacks and social phobias are still present, treatment with a tricyclic antidepressant and/or behavioral therapy may be instituted. On the other hand, all patients with primary alcoholism should be questioned about panic disorder, agoraphobia, and social phobias. If these disorders co-occur with alcoholism, the patient should be reassessed after detoxification and alcohol treatment. If these disorders are not alleviated with alcohol treatment alone, specific psychopharmacologic and psychotherapeutic measures should be instituted.

Generalized Anxiety Disorder

Patients with generalized anxiety disorder (GAD) have unrealistic or excessive worry about one or more life circumstances for 6 months or longer during which they are bothered more days than not by these concerns (Exhibit 7). The patient must also have at least 6 of 18 symptoms from three categories:

Exhibit 7. Diagnostic criteria for generalized anxiety disorder

A. Unrealistic or excessive anxiety and worry (apprehensive expectation) about two or more life circumstances, e.g., worry about possible
misfortune to one's child (who is in no danger) and worry about fi-
nances (for no good reason), for a period of 6 months or longer, during which the person has been bothered more days than not by these
concerns. In children and adolescents, this may take the form of anxiety and worry about academic, athletic, and social performance.

B. If another Axis I disorder is present, the focus of the anxiety and
worry in A is unrelated to it, e.g., the anxiety or worry is not about
having a panic attack (as in panic disorder), being embarrassed in public (as in social phobia), being contaminated (as in obsessive-compulsive disorder), or gaining weight (as in anorexia nervosa).

C. The disturbance does not occur only during the course of a mood
disorder or a psychotic disorder.

D. At least 6 of the following 18 symptoms are often present when anxious (do not include symptoms present only during panic attacks):

Motor tension
1. trembling, twitching, or feeling shaky
2. muscle tension, aches, or soreness
3. restlessness
4. easy fatigability

Autonomic hyperactivity
5. shortness of breath or smothering sensations
6. palpitations or accelerated heart rate (tachycardia)
7. sweating or cold clammy hands
8. dry mouth
9. dizziness or lightheadedness
10. nausea, diarrhea, or other abdominal distress
11. flushes (hot flashes) or chills
12. frequent urination
13. trouble swallowing or "lump in throat"

Vigilance and scanning
14. feeling keyed up or on edge
15. exaggerated startle response
16. difficulty concentrating or "mind going blank" because of
anxiety
17. trouble falling or staying asleep
18. irritability

E. It cannot be established that an organic factor initiated and maintained the disturbance, e.g., hyperthyroidism, caffeine intoxication.

Source: Reprinted with permission from the *Diagnostic and Statistical Manual of Mental Disorders.
Third Edition, Revised.* Copyright 1987 American Psychiatric Association, p. 252-253.

(1) motor tension, (2) autonomic hyperactivity, and (3) vigilance and scanning. In some patients, symptoms of GAD are lifelong and persistent, whereas for other patients, the symptoms are acute, intermittent, and closely related to stressful life events.

In primary care, the majority of patients with symptoms of GAD develop these symptoms secondary to another major DSM-III-R disorder, most commonly panic disorder, major depression, or alcohol abuse (Breslau and Davis 1985; Katon et al. 1987*b*). These three disorders must be actively screened for and ruled out along with organic causes of anxiety (see Chapter 8). This will leave only a small group of patients with generalized anxiety disorder. Recent research suggests that many of these GAD patients actually do have infrequent panic attacks (Barlow et al. 1986; Katon et al. 1987*b*) and, similar to patients with panic disorder, may respond better, especially over the course of several months, to tricyclic antidepressants than standard benzodiazepines (Johnstone et al. 1980; Kahn et al. 1986). Other proven psychopharmacologic agents for GAD include benzodiazepines, beta-blockers, and buspirone (Roy-Byrne and Katon 1987).

Social Phobia

The central feature of social phobia is a persistent fear of, and compelling desire to avoid, a situation in which the individual is exposed to public scrutiny and may act in a way that will be humiliating and embarrassing (APA 1987). Examples include being unable to urinate in a public lavatory, hand trembling when writing in the presence of others, and saying foolish things or not being able to answer questions in social situations. To fit this diagnosis, the patient must not only fear social situations, but actually avoid them or endure them with intense anxiety. These avoidant behaviors interfere with social or occupational functioning and the patient has marked distress about being afraid. Other DSM-III-R disorders, such as panic disorder or major depression, must be ruled out, and the fear must be unrelated to symptoms that are actually caused by a medical disorder (e.g., trembling or tremor in benign essential tremor). One of the few studies of treatment of social phobias (Roy-Byrne and Katon 1987) reported convincing evidence of the superiority of MAOIs in 70 percent of cases and suggested that beta-blockers were no better than placebos. No reports of tricyclic antidepressant efficacy have been published. Exposure-based behavioral treatments (reviewed in Chapter 10) have been reported to be successful (Heimberg et al. 1985).

Simple Phobia

Simple phobia refers to a persistent fear of and compelling desire to avoid a circumscribed stimuli (object or situation) other than fear of having a panic attack (panic disorder) or humiliation or embarrassment in certain social situations (as in social phobia) (APA 1987). Also, the phobic stimulus must be unrelated to the content of the obsessions in obsessive-compulsive disorder or the trauma of posttraumatic stress disorder. The person recognizes the fear as excessive or unreasonable, but nonetheless avoids the situation or endures it with intense anxiety. Exposure to the object (dog, cat, snake) or to the situation (heights, closed-in spaces) invariably brings on intense anxiety, and the avoidance interferes with the patient's life.

Systematic desensitization and in vivo exposure are the most effective treatments for the simple phobias, and no real benefit has ever been shown from medications (Roy-Byrne and Katon 1987).

Posttraumatic Stress Disorder

The DSM-III-R criteria (APA 1987) for PTSD are presented in Exhibit 8. Patients with PTSD have experienced a severe catastrophic event that is outside the range of normal human experience and would be distressing to anyone. The patient frequently and persistently reexperiences the event by having recurrent, often intrusive images of the trauma; recurrent dreams or nightmares of the event; suddenly acting or feeling as if the traumatic event were reoccurring, including illusions, hallucinations, or flashback episodes; and intense psychologic distress when exposed to environmental stimuli that symbolize or resemble an aspect of the traumatic event. Patients with PTSD have persistent avoidance of stimuli associated with the trauma or numbing of general responsiveness, as well as chronic symptoms of increased arousal when exposed to events that symbolize or resemble an aspect of the traumatic event. Recent research has suggested that patients with PTSD have increased autonomic nervous system tone. Vietnam veterans with PTSD were found to have chronic elevation of noradrenergic activity compared with veterans having other psychiatric diagnoses (Kosten et al. 1987). Kolb (1984) also showed that combat veterans with PTSD had greater autonomic nervous system arousal in response to an audiotape of battle sounds than did combat veterans without the disorder.

Panic disorder is also believed to be secondary to dyscontrol of the central alarm system of the brain that controls the autonomic nervous system, and researchers have reported strong links between panic disorder and PTSD. Mellman and Davis (1985) found that 25 of 25 Vietnam veterans with PTSD reported that their flashbacks occurred during anxiety states meeting DSM-III criteria for panic attacks. Rainey and colleagues (1987) administered infusions of sodium lactate (which cause panic in approximately 70 percent of panic attack patients versus less than 5 percent of controls) to seven patients with PTSD, six of whom also met criteria for panic disorder. The lactate infusions resulted in flashbacks in all seven patients and panic attacks in six patients.

Exhibit 8.   Diagnostic criteria for posttraumatic stress disorder

A. The person has experienced an event that is outside the range of usual human experience and that would be markedly distressing to almost anyone, e.g., serious threat to one's life or physical integrity; serious threat or harm to one's children, spouse, or other close relatives and friends; sudden destruction of one's home or community; or seeing another person who has recently been, or is being, seriously injured or killed as the result of an accident or physical violence.

B. The traumatic event is persistently reexperienced in at least one of the following ways:
    1. recurrent and intrusive distressing recollections of the event (in young children, repetitive play in which themes or aspects of the trauma are expressed)
    2. recurrent distressing dreams of the event
    3. sudden acting or feeling as if the traumatic event were recurring (includes a sense of reliving the experience, illusions, hallucinations, and dissociative [flashback] episodes, even those that occur upon awakening or when intoxicated)
    4. intense psychological distress at exposure to events that symbolize or resemble an aspect of the traumatic event, including anniversaries of the trauma.

C. Persistent avoidance of stimuli associated with the trauma or numbing of general responsiveness (not present before the trauma), as indicated by at least three of the following:
    1. efforts to avoid thoughts or feelings associated with the trauma
    2. efforts to avoid activities or situations that arouse recollections of the trauma
    3. inability to recall an important aspect of the trauma (psychogenic amnesia)
    4. markedly diminished interest in significant activities (in young children, loss of recently acquired developmental skills such as toilet training or language skills)
    5. feeling of detachment or estrangement from others
    6. restricted range of affect, e.g., unable to have loving feelings
    7. sense of a foreshortened future, e.g., does not expect to have a career, marriage, or children, or a long life.

D. Persistent symptoms of increased arousal (not present before the trauma), as indicated by at least two of the following:
    1. difficulty falling or staying asleep
    2. irritability or outbursts of anger

Exhibit 8. (continued)

3. difficulty concentrating
4. hypervigilance
5. exaggerated startle response
6. physiologic reactivity upon exposure to events that symbolize or resemble an aspect of the traumatic event (e.g., a woman who was raped in an elevator breaks out in a sweat when entering any elevator).

E. Duration of the disturbance (symptoms in B, C, and D) of at least 1 month. Specify delayed onset if the onset of symptoms was at least 6 months after the trauma.

Source: Reprinted with permission from the *Diagnostic and Statistical Manual of Mental Disorders. Third Edition, Revised.* Copyright 1987 American Psychiatric Association, p. 250-251.

If there is a connection between PTSD and panic disorder, then medications that are effective in dampening autonomic nervous system tone in panic disorder should be effective in PTSD. Recent reports suggest that both imipramine and MAOIs are effective in PTSD (Bleich et al. 1986), and Kolb and associates (1984) demonstrated that clonidine, an alpha-2 receptor agonist that diminishes release of norepinephrine, has also been effective in reducing the autonomic hyperactivity of PTSD.

In primary care, civilian cases of PTSD are occasionally seen, and these patients may have combinations of symptoms of PTSD, panic disorder, and major depression (Figure 2). These cases are often precipitated by extreme

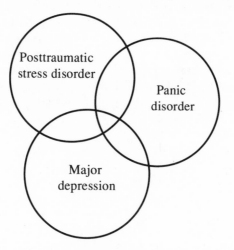

Figure 2. Relationship of posttraumatic stress disorder to panic disorder and major depression.

trauma such as a severe automobile accident, industrial accident, or natural disaster (flood, hurricane, fire). Many of these cases are complicated by the legal and disability systems that may unconsciously lead to prolongation of disability.·Early intervention with accurate diagnosis and aggressive treatment is essential to avoid the risk of long-term disability.

The following case demonstrates the overlap between PTSD, panic disorder, and major depression and the reinforcement of maladaptive illness behavior by the disability system.

Posttraumatic Stress Disorder

Mrs. R was a 38-year-old mother of two employed as a food service worker in a local hospital. Her problems started when she wheeled her food service cart into an elevator that malfunctioned and fell two floors. Mrs. R fell down striking her head and neck and was unconscious for an undetermined amount of time. The elevator lights went out when it malfunctioned, and she was trapped inside for 1 to 2 hours while an elevator maintenance crew worked to get her out. She was hospitalized for several days, and a neurologic evaluation including CT head scan, skull x rays, and spinal films proved negative. After the accident, she developed chronic neck and head pain as well as nightmares of the incident and daytime intrusive memories and flashbacks. She felt she could never go back to work at the same hospital because of severe anxiety associated with even passing the building. She refused to use elevators because of severe anxiety and wondered if she could ever do the same type of work again. She complained of insomnia, decreased energy, irritability and depressed mood, anhedonia, poor concentration, and poor appetite since the accident. In addition, she developed acute attacks of rapid heartbeat, diaphoresis, dyspnea, dizziness, paresthesia, and a sense of impending doom. These attacks were very frightening to her and made her fearful of going out alone. Her husband complained that she was detached from him and the children since the accident and was ignoring most of her household duties.

The patient was diagnosed as having PTSD, panic disorder, and major depression. She was started on imipramine, 50 mg daily, with dosage increasing to 250 mg over 2 to 3 weeks. Most of her symptoms improved rapidly on this medication, but she still felt she could never return to her old job and eventually was given 50-percent disability retirement in a legal settlement.

Chapter 7

Comorbidity With Medical Disorders

Two major questions are examined in this chapter. First, how does panic disorder affect the course of chronic medical disorders afflicting the patient? Second, does panic disorder predispose the patient to specific medical disorders?

As discussed in Chapter 9, scientists have hypothesized that panic disorder results from central dyscontrol of the brain alarm system that warns the patient about external dangers. The locus ceruleus, a cluster of noradrenergic neurons located in the pons, may be the central control mechanism for the autonomic nervous system (Redmond 1979). Activation of the locus ceruleus has been associated with fear and alarm reactions in primates (Redmond et al. 1976). Moreover, bilateral lesions of the locus ceruleus in animals lead to failure to show normal cardioaccelerator responses (increased pulse and blood pressure) to threatening stimuli (Snyder et al. 1977).

The locus ceruleus has projections to many regions of the brain associated with responses to fear and pain. It also has projections to the cerebral cortex which, as Svensson (1987) emphasized, might be involved with the interpretation of "meaning" or relevance of a stimulus to the individual. Finally, the locus ceruleus has projections to limbic areas, such as the amygdala, which are important regions for emotional and cardiovascular control.

Activation of the locus ceruleus appears critical to the defense reaction that mobilizes an individual for the "fight or flight" response (Svensson 1987). This reaction involves increased vigilance and fear, neurogenic activity of sympathetic fibers to the heart, splanchnic region, and kidneys, central suppression of vagal restraint of the heart, and an ensuing blood pressure elevation mainly caused by increased cardiac output. The sympathetic activation of the kidneys is associated with increased renin release and activation of the renin-aldosterone axis as well as mobilization of glucocorticoids.

Figure 3 depicts the multiple connections between the autonomic nervous system and the peripheral organ systems. Panic disorder may be caused by dysregulation of the locus ceruleus causing the initiation of fight-or-flight reactions at inappropriate times, i.e., when there is no symbolic or actual danger (Charney et al. 1984). When panic disorder or major depression is associated with chronic medical illness, the psychiatric illness causes amplifi-

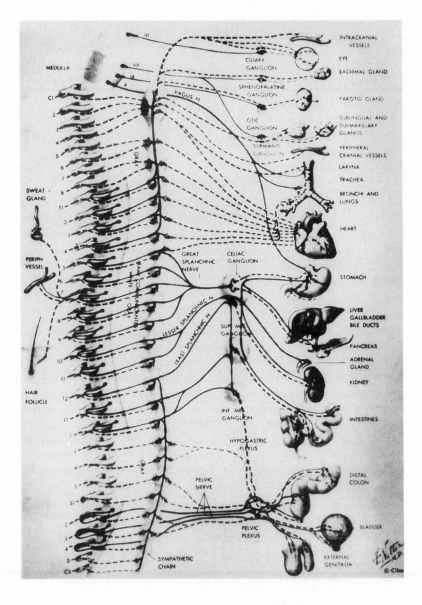

Figure 3. Autonomic nervous system. Source: The CIBA Collection of Medical Illustrations, by Frank H. Netter, M.D. Volume I, Plate 54. Copyright 1962 by CIBA-GEIGY Corporation. Reproduced with permission. All rights reserved.

cation of symptomatic complaints of the medical illness, such as increased reports of angina in the patient with chronic angina pectoris and panic disorder (Bridges and Goldberg 1985). This worsening of symptoms is probably secondary to both the increased tendency to report symptoms and a worsening of physiologic illness secondary to sympathetic nervous system arousal. For example, in a patient with angina pectoris and severe coronary artery disease, the increased sympathetic arousal accompanying a panic attack could cause increased heart rate, blood pressure, and cardiac output, potentially precipitating a bout of angina pectoris. These patients may present with increased chest pain after being controlled in the past on cardiac medications such as beta-blockers, nitrates, or calcium channel blockers. A vicious cycle of symptoms may ensue, with panic attacks provoking angina and anginal episodes provoking panic. In these cases, once the panic disorder is effectively treated, the chest pain episodes may decrease.

Noyes and colleagues (1980) addressed the association of panic disorder with specific medical illnesses by following patients with panic disorder and a surgical outpatient control group over a 6-year period, comparing the incidence of six illnesses thought to have a psychophysiologic basis. Patients with panic disorder were found to have a significantly higher rate of hypertension and peptic ulcer disease over this period. Katon (1984) also found that 55 primary care patients with panic disorder had a significantly higher rate of

---

Panic Disorder Associated With Angina Pectoris

A 60-year-old male treated with propranolol for angina pectoris began to visit his physician with increased frequency due to worsening angina. Calcium channel blockers and long-acting nitrates were prescribed, but they did not decrease the anginal episodes. Prior to referring the patient for repeat angiography, psychiatric consultation was obtained because the patient had had a marked increase in nervousness and anxiety. The patient revealed severe financial problems necessitating filing for bankruptcy and problems with the recent divorce of his daughter. Acute episodes of shortness of breath, chest tightness, dyspnea, tremulousness, and dizziness had been occurring for the last 2 months, often preceding more typical episodes of substernal chest pain radiating into his left arm. He had become increasingly afraid to go out unaccompanied by his wife because of these episodes, and he had become progressively more isolated socially because the episodes seemed to occur more often when in groups or crowds of people.

He was diagnosed as having panic disorder and started on imipramine, 25 mg per day, increasing by 25 mg every 3 days. On a total dosage of 75 mg, his panic episodes disappeared and his angina was once again well controlled on his original regime. He remained well over a 1-year period.

peptic ulcer disease (diagnosed by endoscopy) and hypertension than did clinic controls. In a second epidemiologic study of panic disorder in primary care, Katon (1986) found that 13.6 percent of primary care patients with panic disorder had hypertension versus 4.4 percent of controls (p = .03) but did not find a higher prevalence of peptic ulcer disease.

Clinically, patients often have labile hypertension during active panic attacks, but once these attacks are blocked by psychopharmacologic agents, the labile hypertension usually subsides (Balon et al. 1988; Freedman et al. 1985; Shear 1986). The possibility that panic disorder may be causal in the development of hypertension is further suggested by the fact that 17 of 22 patients in the Noyes et al. (1980) study developed hypertension 2 or more years after they developed panic disorder. An intriguing biologic finding also supports this hypothesis. Several research groups have found significantly higher resting levels of epinephrine in arteriolized venous blood in patients with panic disorder versus controls (Villacres et al. 1987; Nesse et al. 1984; Appleby et al. 1981). A subset of hypertensives also have higher epinephrine

---

Panic Disorder Associated With Labile Hypertension

Mr. S was a 28-year-old laborer and fishing guide who presented with an acute episode of chest pain, tachycardia, "head rushes," and labile hypertension. His blood pressure often went up as high as 200/115 with these episodes. Over a 6-month period, he was hospitalized three times for these symptoms. Cardiac enzymes, treadmill test, and echocardiogram revealed only mitral valve prolapse. He was started on atenolol 50 mg twice a day, but this did not relieve his symptoms.

He was referred to an endocrinologist for the acute episodes of chest pain and labile hypertension. Separate workups for pheochromocytoma, carcinoid, and thyroid disease were negative.

Over the 6-month period, he lost his job and had to apply for welfare and ran up $10,000 in medical bills. He was finally referred for psychiatric consultation where he revealed that the acute episodes of chest pain were accompanied by rapid heart beat, sweatiness, dizziness, shortness of breath, tingling in hands and feet, and a sense of impending doom. He also suffered from irritability, insomnia, anorexia, 40-pound weight loss, and lack of pleasure in his usual activities.

He was diagnosed as meeting criteria for panic disorder and major depression and was started on imipramine, 50 mg daily increasing to 250 mg, and he rapidly recovered over a 1-month period. He started back to work in a lumber mill and worked steadily for the succeeding year. His labile hypertension resolved completely, and he was able to taper and discontinue his atenolol over a 1-month period.

levels than controls, and chronically high epinephrine levels may lead to chronic peripheral vasoconstriction over time (Weder and Julius 1985).

Studies of patients with panic disorder referred to psychopharmacologic trials in anxiety disorder clinics found no increase in hypertension in these patients, so the above findings may be specific to patients with panic disorder who frequently visit primary care physicians. Future research questions that need to be addressed include: Is there a subgroup of patients with panic disorder who have labile hypertension initially as a result of hyperactive central noradrenergic mechanisms involving the locus ceruleus who are not adequately treated and then develop chronic hypertension? Does the labile hypertension, locus ceruleus, and sympathetic nervous system hyperactivity and high peripheral epinephrine levels cause long-term irreversible peripheral vasoconstriction leading to chronic hypertension in these patients?

Cardiovascular Morbidity and Mortality

Existing studies of associations between panic disorder and cardiovascular morbidity and mortality are all retrospective. In two independent studies, Coryell and colleagues (1982, 1986) found an increased mortality for male panic disorder patients, the increase being accounted for by cardiovascular death and suicide. These results were based on small numbers of expected and observed deaths. In the first study, six men were expected to die and 12 men died; in the second, 1.8 total male deaths were expected and four men actually died, three from cardiovascular causes. In three other studies of "neurotic patients," some of whom had panic disorder, no link between neurotic illness and cardiovascular morbidity was found (Martin et al. 1985; Black et al. 1985; Winokur and Black 1987).

One last study associating panic disorder with cardiovascular morbidity (Kahn et al. 1987) reported that patients with idiopathic cardiomyopathy had an increased prevalence of panic disorder (51 percent definite panic disorder, 31 percent probable panic disorder) compared to cardiac patients with post-infarction cardiac failure (5.5 percent definite and 17 percent probable panic disorder) and patients with rheumatic or congenital heart disease (0 percent definite or probable panic disorder). All patients were awaiting transplants, and in most patients, the panic disorder preceded the symptoms of idiopathic cardiomyopathy. The authors noted that both ectopic atrial tachyarrhythmias (Gillette et al. 1985) and catecholamine-secreting pheochromocytomas (Van Vliet et al. 1966) can cause myocarditis and cardiomyopathy and hypothesized that either autonomically induced small-vessel changes or high catecholamine levels that may be associated with panic disorder could lead similarly to myocarditis and progressive cardiomyopathy in some patients with panic disorder (Kahn et al. 1987). Clearly, this study needs to be replicated, but the results are intriguing.

Panic Disorder and Mitral Valve Prolapse

MVP refers to a condition in which the leaflets of the mitral valve are redundant and sag toward the left atrial chamber during ventricular systole (Dager et al. 1986). This sagging, with sudden tensing of the submitral apparatus, results in auscultatory findings of one or more systolic clicks and the presence of a mid-to-late systolic murmur of mitral regurgitation (Devereux et al. 1976). Maneuvers that decrease left ventricular volume (such as abrupt standing or inhalation of amyl nitrate vapors) increase leaflet redundancy and may unmask occult MVP. Clinical symptoms of MVP include atypical chest pain, dyspnea, tachycardia, palpitations, light-headedness, syncope, fatigue, and anxiety (Barlow et al. 1968; Devereux et al. 1976). Reported complications included sudden death, progressive mitral regurgitation, and bacterial endocarditis (Wynne 1986). These signs and symptoms and their complications have been called the MVP syndrome (Devereux et al. 1976).

MVP is a controversial syndrome with highly variable prevalence rates reported in the general population, conflicting studies reporting prevalence of complications and autonomic defects, and various criteria used to define the "disease" (Wynne 1986; Margraf et al. 1988). Thus, reported prevalence rates have ranged between 5 and 21 percent. Much of this variability is due to the different criteria used for diagnosis. As Dager and colleagues (1986) emphasized, the diagnosis of MVP still has no "gold standard." The changes in mitral valve mobility are in reality continuous, not dichotomous variables (Wynne 1986). The continuum of changes includes on the one end a near "flail" leaflet and florid mitral regurgitation and on the other equivocal, nonspecific thickening with minor abnormalities of valve closure and no corroborative physical findings. The former severe abnormality may be associated with connective tissue disorders such as Marfan's or Ehlers-Danlos syndromes (Wynne 1986).

Different studies of prevalence have used different criteria for diagnosis. In one study, the prevalence dropped from 13 to 0.5 percent when more stringent criteria were employed (Warth et al. 1985). Most of the older studies used M-mode echocardiography, which may be subject to serious methodologic errors leading to false positive and negative findings (Dager et al. 1986; Margraf et al. 1988). The more recent 2-D echocardiographic studies provide a cross-sectional representation of cardiac structure and valve leaflet anatomy and are considered much more accurate tests. However, there is still no consensus among cardiologists regarding the minimum extent of mitral valve leaflet sagging required to make the diagnosis, especially in the absence of the corroborative physical findings. Thus, while echocardiography is considered a more sensitive test to detect MVP than is auscultation, there is also great variability in the criteria to detect MVP as well as the application of these criteria (Wynne 1986; Dager et al. 1986; Margraf et al. 1988). Recent estimates of the retest and interrater reliability of raters from the same laboratory using the same criteria have demonstrated a lack of diagnostic precision (Margraff et al. 1988; Dager et al. 1986). Reliability from raters from different institutions is even less. Thus, Gorman and colleagues (1986*b*) demonstrated that in a series of 15 patients with panic disorder, one rater diagnosed MVP in 9 patients while a second did not make the diagnosis in a single patient.

A recent editorial by Wynne (1986) suggested that two groups of subjects carry the diagnosis of MVP. The first consists of persons in whom the disorder is principally an echocardiographic finding. These people are no more symptomatic than controls, have no more arrhythmias, and are often free of the typical auscultory findings and have a low risk of complications. The echocardiographic findings in this group are probably normal variants and reflect the technologic advances in defining valve motion, while emphasizing the difficulty in differentiating variants of normal valve mobility. The second group consists of patients who typically not only have evidence of prolapse on echocardiography but who also have clinical findings of mitral valve regurgitation (with or without a systolic click). These people may have symptoms related to valvular insufficiency and appear to have an increased risk of infective endocarditis as well as progressive mitral regurgitation. Two useful markers have been identified to help differentiate between the first group (with trivial MVP) and the second group (with important MVP): (1) the degree of redundancy of the valve, a finding that can be defined echocardiographically and (2) the presence of mitral regurgitation on physical examination (Wynne 1986). Thus, Nishimura and colleagues (1985) recently found that almost every patient with a complication of MVP had redundant valves as indicated by an increase in mitral valve leaflet thickness of 5 mm or more. Even in this group, the complications of endocarditis or cerebral embolism averaged less than 1 percent per year. These complications tend to occur in older patients and in males.

Do patients with mitral valve prolapse have higher rates of panic disorder? Margraf and colleagues (1988) recently reviewed the eight studies in the world's literature that asked this question and reported no elevated prevalence of panic disorder in MVP patients compared to subjects with other cardiac complaints. However, both patients with MVP and control patients in a cardiac practice had a higher prevalence of panic attacks than did controls with MVP who were not seeking medical help. These data suggest that patients with MVP and panic are most likely to seek medical help, probably secondary to the symptoms caused by severe anxiety.

Margraf and colleagues (1988) also reviewed the world's literature on MVP in patients with panic disorder. They pointed out the many methodologic problems in these studies including lack of control groups in all but five studies, lack of blinded raters for the psychiatric diagnosis, and lack of homogeneous samples (some included depressive or generalized anxiety disorder patients). Eighteen percent of the patients with panic disorder or agoraphobia in 17 studies met definite criteria for MVP, and 27 percent met criteria for probable MVP versus an average rate of definite MVP of 1 percent in normal controls and probable or definite MVP in 12 percent. In the 11 studies that allowed an estimate of subjects that met both auscultory and echocardiographic criteria, 10 percent of the patients with panic disorder met criteria for MVP versus 2 percent of the controls—a highly significant difference.

In a recent study (Gorman et al. 1988b) with normal controls, raters blinded to psychiatric diagnoses, and severity of MVP scored as mild, moderate, and severe, 14 of 36 (39 percent) patients with panic disorder or agoraphobia met criteria for MVP versus 4 of 22 (18 percent) normal controls (p < .05). However, the MVP in the patients with panic or agoraphobia was mild and not associated with thickened mitral leaflets (the high-risk group for complications described by Nishimura and colleagues [1985] had an increase in mitral-valve thickness to 5mm or more) or small ventricular size. The authors concluded that MVP is more common in patients with panic disorder or agoraphobia, but is of doubtful significance.

Patients with panic disorder and MVP respond to antipanic drugs as well as patients with panic disorder alone (Gorman et al. 1981a; Grunhaus et al. 1984). Moreover, lactate infusion affects patients with panic disorder or agoraphobia identically whether or not MVP is present (Gorman et al. 1981b). Gorman and associates (1988b) have now reported several cases of patients with panic disorder and echocardiographically proven MVP in which the echocardiograms became normal after the panic attacks had been in remission for more than 6 months.

These findings suggest that panic disorder with MVP and panic disorder without MVP are the same illness and that panic attacks may actually be causing MVP in some patients. Gorman and colleagues (1988b) suggested that the type of MVP seen with panic disorder is mild, much like the echocardiographic variant of normal described by Wynne (1986), and that the tachycardia and adrenergic discharge associated with panic attacks may cause a temporary anatomical deformation of the mitral valve or desynchrony in ventricular contraction sufficient to produce mild echocardiographic MVP. Experimental evidence shows that mild MVP can be induced by high heart rate and low ventricular volume (Ballenger et al. 1986) or by direct ventricular stimulation (Rosenthal et al. 1985).

Ballenger (1986) also hypothesized that high levels of circulating catecholamines in the presence of high heart rates can result in MVP. Supporting evidence for panic disorder and resulting high heart rates and adrenergic discharge causing MVP was provided by Channick et al. (1981), who found that 40 percent of patients with hyperthyroidism also had MVP.

A review of all these findings suggests that while panic disorder is associated with an increased prevalence of MVP, it seems to be a mild type of MVP that is principally an echocardiographic finding. It has little clinical relevance

Panic Disorder and MVP

Mrs. D was a 34-year-old medical student who had been having episodes of palpitations and atypical chest pain for 6 months. She had a normal physical exam and electrocardiogram, but an echocardiogram revealed mitral valve prolapse. She was treated with 50 mg of atenolol twice a day, which decreased her symptoms slightly. Because of her apparent anxiety, she was referred for psychiatric consultation.

On psychiatric interview, the patient revealed that her episodes of palpitations and chest pain were accompanied by dyspnea, dizziness, paresthesia, and gastrointestinal cramping. She had suffered episodes like this 5 years before and was diagnosed as having "colitis" and treated with antispasmodics. Mrs. D revealed increasing social phobias since her attacks began, with fear of crowds and of eating in restaurants. She also described her father as a nervous phobic person who never went anywhere without her mother.

The patient was diagnosed as having panic disorder and mitral valve prolapse and was started on desipramine 25 mg with the dosage increased to 75 mg over 10 days. She made a rapid recovery, with complete amelioration of panic attacks and the episodes of atypical chest pain and palpitations. The atenolol was successfully tapered and discontinued after 3 weeks.

and does not require prophylactic antibiotic treatment. It may be caused by increased heart rate and catecholamine excretion and adrenergic tone. Weissman and colleagues' (1987) findings supported this conclusion. They found that patients with MVP alone differed from patients with MVP and panic disorder and from patients with panic disorder alone. Patients with MVP alone exhibited more syncope, more orthostatic hypotension during quiet standing, loss of normal age-related decrease in vagally medicated heart rate variability during deep breathing, and lower 24-hour epinephrine excretion. In contrast, patients with panic attacks with or without MVP had greater increases in heart rate and mean blood pressure during each minute of quiet standing and during the early strain phase of the Valsalva maneuver.

Panic disorder is frequently unrecognized in a patient with panic disorder and mitral valve prolapse. Many of these patients are prescribed beta-blockers for the MVP, which usually only mildly decrease the severe anxiety and may precipitate or worsen depressive symptoms. A switch to more specific treatment with a tricyclic antidepressant, benzodiazepine, or MAOI usually leads to rapid amelioration of panic attacks and enables the clinician to also discontinue the beta-blocker.

Chapter 8

Medical Differential Diagnosis

In medical patients with severe anxiety, the physician must initially focus on any chronic medical illness that could precipitate anxiety (temporal lobe epilepsy, hypoglycemic episodes in a diabetic, paroxysmal atrial tachycardia in a patient with Wolff-Parkinson-White syndrome) as well as review all pharmacologic agents that the patient is taking that could cause anxiety either as a side effect of normal therapeutic levels or as a marker of toxic blood levels (Rosenbaum 1982). For instance, an asthmatic with a toxic aminophylline serum level and a diabetic with recently increased insulin dosage may both suffer from symptoms that simulate anxiety attacks.

Mackenzie and Popkin (1983) have suggested the term "organic anxiety syndrome" for anxiety symptoms that are found on history, physical examination, or laboratory tests to be secondary to an organic disease, medication, or drugs and where there is no clouding of consciousness (as in delirium), no loss of cognitive function (as in dementia), no predominant disturbance in mood (as in organic affective syndrome), and no hallucinations or delusions (as in organic delusional syndrome or organic hallucinosis).

Medical disorders known to be associated with anxiety are listed in Exhibit 9. Among this list of disorders, the medical illnesses that can cause symptoms most resembling panic disorder include hyperthyroidism, cardiac arrhythmias, mitral valve prolapse, hypoglycemic episodes, temporal lobe epilepsy, pheochromocytoma, caffeinism, pulmonary embolus, electrolyte abnormalities, Cushing's Syndrome, and menopausal symptoms. This review focuses on thyroid disease, hypoglycemia, temporal lobe epilepsy, and pheochromocytoma and their differential diagnoses with panic disorder. This chapter also discusses the importance of marijuana, cocaine, amphetamines, and other street drugs in occasionally precipitating the onset of panic disorder and the mimicking of panic disorder by withdrawal from central nervous system depressants and opiates.

Thyroid Disease and Panic Disorder

Klein, in his classic 1964 paper on panic disorder, hypothesized that panic patients fell into two groups: (1) a younger group, age 20 to 40, who develop

Exhibit 9. Medical disorders and substances that can mimic panic symptoms

Alcohol withdrawal	Hyperparathyroidism
Amphetamines	Hyperthyroidism
Asthma	Hypoglycemia
Caffeinism	Hypothyroidism
Cardiac arrhythmias	Marijuana
Cardiomyopathies	Menopausal symptoms
Cocaine	Mitral valve prolapse
Coronary artery disease	Pheochromocytoma
Cushing's syndrome	Pulmonary embolus
Drug withdrawal	Temporal lobe epilepsy
Electrolyte abnormalities	True vertigo

panic attacks in association with an acute life event, often separation from a significant other, and (2) an older group who develop panic disorder in conjunction with a medical illness, especially an illness with apparent hormonal fluctuations.

No definite proof of this division of patients by age of onset and precipitating factors has developed, but there is continued interest in hormonal relationships to panic disorder. Thyroid disease has been mentioned most frequently. Several case report series have described both generalized anxiety and panic disorder developing secondary to hyperthyroidism (Katerndahl and Vande Creek 1986; Turner 1984). Patients with hyperthyroidism often experience anxiety, tachycardia, palpitations, sweating, dyspnea, irritability, diarrhea, and diffuse anxiety (Lesser et al. 1987). Lindemann and colleagues (1984) found, in a retrospective study of 295 panic disorder patients, a high prevalence of thyroid disorders (9.2 percent), based on patient self-reports. Katon and colleagues (unpublished data) also found a significantly higher prevalence of thyroid disease in patients with panic disorder than in controls in a primary care clinic, based on physician reports. However, three recent studies failed to find evidence of abnormally increased thyroid hormone levels in panic disorder patients (Yeragani et al. 1987; Lesser et al. 1987; Stein and Uhde 1988).

One study did show that panic disorder patients had significantly higher levels of free T_3 and T_4 (Adams et al. 1985), although these levels were still in the normal range. Fishman and colleagues (1985) demonstrated a high incidence of very low thyroid stimulating hormone (TSH) levels. Taken together, these two studies suggest a relative increase in thyroid function in patients with panic disorder. This relative (but not abnormal) increase would be consistent with the hypothesized increase in adrenergic activity in panic disorder patients, which could increase the synthesis of thyroid hormone (Roy-Byrne et al. 1988). Consistent with this possibility are three studies that found reduced or blunted TSH responses to thyroid releasing hormone TRH in panic disorder patients (Roy-Byrne et al. 1986; Hamlin and Pottash 1986; Hamlin 1987) and also in a subgroup of depressed patients (Roy-Byrne et al. 1988).

The above data suggest that the majority of patients with panic disorder are euthyroid, but may have some abnormalities of their hypophyseal-pituitary-thyroid axis secondary to increased noradrenergic central activity. These changes are probably not clinically important. Slight elevation of thyroid hormone levels occur in many acute psychiatric illnesses (psychosis, depression, and anxiety), and these elevations represent a stress response rather than thyroid disease (Nusynowitz and Young 1979).

Overall, patients with panic disorder should have a thyroid screen ordered if they have a history of increased appetite, weight loss, heat intolerance, irradiation of neck and chest, subtotal thyroidectomy or iodine 131 treatment, or physical examination findings of ophthalmopathy, goiter, or hypermetabolic state (Raj and Sheehan 1987).

Hypoglycemia

Hypoglycemia can cause symptoms such as cognitive anxiety, tachycardia, sweating, lightheadedness, tremors, and hunger. It may occur from excess insulin in diabetics, secondary to a prediabetic state, or from other medical disorders, such as insulinoma. Primary care physicians frequently see anxious and depressed patients who wonder if hypoglycemia is a cause of their symptoms. This was particularly true in the 1970s, when many lay books and periodicals warned of the symptoms of hypoglycemia, provoking an editorial in the *New England Journal of Medicine* entitled "Non-hypoglycemia is an epidemic condition" (Yager and Young 1984). The authors described patients who believed they had hypoglycemia but frequently had psychiatric illnesses. The stigmatization of mental illness and the social acceptability of medical illness made the diagnosis of hypoglycemia preferable. This diagnosis enabled patients to deal actively and easily with their symptoms by simply following dietary rituals or prescriptions. Also, a diagnosis of hypoglycemia enabled these patients to attain the sick role, entitling them to increased family and social support.

Hypoglycemia has been carefully studied as a cause of panic disorder, but little supportive evidence has been found. Gorman and Martinez (1984) examined blood glucose in 10 patients with panic disorder during lactate infusion (which precipitates acute anxiety attacks in approximately 70 percent of patients with panic disorder). At the point of panic, the lowest blood sugar reported in any patient was 81 mg/dl. Uhde and colleagues (1984) induced hypoglycemia in nine drug free, panic disorder patients with a standard oral challenge of glucose. Although these patients had quite typical hypoglycemic symptoms of tachycardia, light-headedness, sweating, and free-floating anxiety, they reported their symptoms as different from panic attacks.

The diagnostic criteria for hypoglycemia have been controversial, and the value of the glucose tolerance test (GTT) is limited, because 25 to 48 percent of normal subjects appear to develop hypoglycemia during testing (Raj and Sheehan 1987). Moreover, patients with vague somatic complaints who often have anxiety and/or depression are probably more likely to be referred for a 4-hour glucose tolerance test; a low blood sugar finding is often inappropriately labeled as the cause of their symptoms (Yager and Young 1974; Ford et al. 1976).

The physician should have a high index of suspicion for panic disorder in patients presenting with "hypoglycemia," and the GTT should be reserved for patients with a history of postprandial attacks, panic attacks with accompanying hunger, or gastric surgery or a family or personal history of endocrine adenomas (Raj and Sheehan 1987). The following case demonstrates the patient's misattribution of hypoglycemia as the cause of psychiatric symptoms (panic disorder and major depression).

Panic Disorder and Major Depression Presenting as Hypoglycemia

Mr. J, a 32-year-old carpenter, presented to the family medicine center with a 6-month history of inability to concentrate, insomnia, decreased energy, weakness, and depression, as well as sudden bouts of palpitations, sweating, light-headedness and stomach tightness. He stated he was desperate and that his inability to function at work caused him to quit his job. He attributed all of these symptoms to hypoglycemia. He had read extensively on the subject and gave his physician six typewritten pages of graphs and charts of his eating patterns. He had long lists of foods that caused worsening of his condition and graphs of the times of the day that were associated with symptoms. He admitted he was depressed and anxious, but felt that was secondary to his inability to think and concentrate, which he attributed to the putative hypoglycemia. Mr. J was raised by an alcoholic father after his mother died of abdominal cancer when he was 2 years old. He had a poor job history with multiple job losses that he attributed to the above "physical" problems. He had been married for the last 5 years to a nurse who had had a pituitary tumor for 2 years with well-documented hypoglycemia.

Both the primary care physician and the psychiatric consultant felt that Mr. J had a major depressive disorder and panic disorder. The appropriate treatment was tricyclic antidepressants and/or psychotherapy, but both physicians were doubtful that they could convince the patient to accept the treatment plan owing to his idiosyncratic explanatory model. He was told the following: "Although it's possible that hypoglycemia is a problem, you are managing that as well as possible with your diet. On the other hand, this illness that you have has certainly caused depression and anxiety with the usual vegetative symptoms of insomnia, decreased ability to concentrate, anxiety attacks, anhedonia, and decreased energy. We would recommend a course of antidepressants for these symptoms." The patient was surprised at this diagnosis but agreed to a trial of antidepressants provided his putative hypoglycemia was reassessed with appropriate blood tests. This compromise was agreed to, and a trial of antidepressants was initiated. The patient had a dramatic response within 3 weeks, with a loss of virtually all his symptoms. A new negotiation was then undertaken regarding psychotherapy. Despite further treatment with the antidepressants and therapy, the patient still believed that he had hypoglycemia, but he was no longer as insistent about needing treatment for it and had relaxed his dietary vigilance considerably.

Pheochromocytoma

Pheochromocytoma is a tumor of chromaffin tissue, with 80 percent occurring in one adrenal gland, 10 percent bilaterally, and 10 percent outside of the adrenal gland (Landsberg and Young 1987). These tumors are found in 1/1000 autopsies and are the cause of 0.1 percent of all cases of hypertension. Most occur in women between the ages of 20 to 40 years. They are associated with cholelithiasis in 15 percent of all cases, with multiple endocrine tumors in 10 percent, and with neurofibromatosis in 5 percent (Raj and Sheehan 1987).

The typical clinical features include hypertension (40 percent paroxysmal and 60 percent sustained), palpitations, headache, flushing, and sweating (Raj and Sheehan 1987). Postural hypotension and tachycardia may be noted, and anxiety has been reported as the fourth most common symptom (Manger and Gifford 1982).

Starkman and colleagues (1985) carefully interviewed 17 patients with pheochromocytoma to determine if they experienced anxiety symptoms similar to patients with generalized anxiety disorder or panic disorder. The patients' subjective descriptions of paroxysmal attacks included headache in 13 (76 percent) patients, sweating and restlessness in 9 (53 percent), and nausea, pounding in the chest, shortness of breath, rapid heartbeat, and an empty, tight feeling in the stomach in 8 (47 percent). These patients generally did not describe any feelings of panic, acute anxiety, or terror. The authors found that although 9 of the 17 patients had some physical symptoms of panic attacks, none met DSM-III criteria for panic disorder. Two had definite generalized anxiety. The authors emphasized that anticipatory anxiety, phobic avoidance, and agoraphobia were not found.

The above data suggest that few patients with pheochromocytoma meet criteria for panic disorder, that physical symptoms usually predominate (headache, sweating, restlessness, nausea, tachycardia), and that phobic behavior and avoidance are rare. Given its rarity, pheochromocytoma workups should be considered only if there is a family or individual history of pheochromocytoma, multiple endocrine adenomas, neurofibromatosis, cholelithiasis, panic attacks with predominant throbbing headache, sweating, or flushing, or physical examination findings of neurofibromata, cafe-au-lait spots, postural tachycardia or hypotension, severe hypertension that is paroxysmal or sustained, or abdominal mass (Raj and Sheehan 1987). Problems in differential diagnosis sometimes occur with somatizing patients who minimize or deny psychologic symptoms and stress, or who present with chest pain or headache and have labile hypertension. Finding phobic behavior and avoidance as well as depressive symptoms may help the physician accurately diagnose panic disorder.

Temporal Lobe Epilepsy and Panic Disorder

Temporal lobe epilepsy (TLE) and panic disorder have several features in common. Both disorders may occur paroxysmally without a precipitory event and may be associated with symptoms of terror, fear, and depersonalization or derealization as well as with autonomic symptoms of diaphoresis, flushing, hyperventilation, and tachycardia (Marshall et al. 1983; Raj and Sheehan 1987). Neuropsychiatric studies have demonstrated that stimulation of specific temporal lobe areas may simulate anxiety. Fear, fright, and feelings of déjà vu have been produced by electrical stimulation of the right temporal gyrus. Gloor and colleagues (1982) reported that stimulation of the hippocampus, amygdala, and parahippocampal gyrus produced sensations of fear in humans.

Reports in the neurologic and psychiatric literature describe anxiety attacks associated with underlying mass lesions of the right temporal lobe (Wall et al. 1985; Ghadirian et al. 1986) and occurring after right temporal lobectomy (Wall et al. 1986). A report by Reiman and colleagues (1986) that patients with panic disorder have asymmetry of blood flow in the region of the parahippocampal gyrus on positron emission tomography (PET) scan also suggested that dysfunction of the temporal lobe may be associated with severe anxiety.

Although similarities exist between temporal lobe epilepsy and panic disorder, temporal lobe epilepsy can be differentiated by the loss or altered state of consciousness, the progression into other types of epilepsy (such as grand mal seizures), semipurposeful movements or psychic behavior (déjà vu, jamais vu), or the presence of hallucinations (Raj and Sheehan 1987). Harper and Roth (1962) found that patients with TLE were more likely to have a history of brain trauma, incontinence, and complete loss of consciousness when compared to patients with panic disorder.

Electroencephalograms should not be ordered routinely in patients with panic disorder. They should be reserved for patients with a history of altered consciousness, automatism, head injury, hallucinations, psychic phenomenon with episodes of déjà vu or jamais vu, past seizures, or a neurologic deficit on physical examination (Raj and Sheehan 1987). If either history or physical examination is positive, regular and sleep electroencephalograms and neurologic consultation is indicated. If a neurologic deficit is present, a computed tomography head scan and/or magnetic resonance imaging (MRI) should be considered as well.

Illicit Drug Use

In some patients, the first anxiety attack is precipitated by the use of marijuana, cocaine, amphetamines, or hallucinogens (Hillard and Viewig 1983; Aronson and Craig 1986). The frightening cognitive or somatic symptoms that can occur with the use of these drugs may cause the patient to respond with anxiety to this perceived loss of control. Alternatively, some of the physiologic effects of these agents may stimulate specific brain receptors associated with anxiety. Thus, the sympathomimetic effects of cocaine and amphetamines can cause an anxiety response. Cocaine, for example, causes the acute release and blocks the reuptake of serotonin, norepinephrine, and dopamine (Mule 1984); chronic use depletes them. Aronson and Craig (1986) hypothesized that the chronic cocaine-induced depletion of biogenic amines could alter the equilibrium of the noradrenergic system by reducing the activity of inhibitory inputs. This reduced inhibitory input may make the chronic cocaine user susceptible to panic attacks. Marijuana causes a well-documented increase in heart rate, probably by beta-adrenergic cardiovascular stimulation (Beaconsfield et al. 1972). This side effect may precipitate severe anxiety in patients.

Withdrawal from sedative-hypnotics, alcohol, or opiates can cause symptoms that are difficult to distinguish from anxiety attacks. In most of these cases, historical data (history of alcohol, barbiturate, benzodiazepine, or opiate use) or physical examination findings ("tracks" from intravenous drug use, tremor, or increased pulse and blood pressure) indicate drug use.

Suggested Medical Workup

How much of a medical workup should the physician complete prior to making a definitive diagnosis of panic disorder? Generally, a thorough biopsychosocial history and physical examination are adequate to make the diagnosis in most patients. This is especially true in the typical case of a relatively young patient (age 18–40) who develops classic anxiety attack symptoms, avoidance behavior, and perhaps depressive symptoms in the context of one or more stressful life events.

Many primary care patients present with somatic symptoms and minimize stressors. In these patients, a brief laboratory screen (complete blood count, blood chemistry panel, and thyroid function tests) in addition to a careful history and physical examination is adequate. This brief screen reassures patients that the clinician has taken their symptoms seriously and has ruled out potential medical problems. It is useful for clinicians to advise these patients prior to the laboratory screen that they believe their symptoms to be secondary to an autonomic nervous system disorder (panic disorder), but that laboratory tests will be useful to exclude medical problems.

At times, a patient's focus on a specific complaint, such as chest pain, dizziness, or epigastric pain or worsening of a medical problem, will necessitate further testing (electrocardiogram, caloric testing, or upper GI series). The clinician must realize the advantages and disadvantages of doing multiple laboratory tests. While tests may accentuate the patient's hypochondriacal tendencies, the additional testing may also decrease patient and physician anxiety about missing a serious illness. Some patients may have both a medical diagnosis and panic disorder, and successful treatment of the medical disorder may still leave a residual panic disorder (Katon and Roy-Byrne 1989).

Chapter 9

Psychobiology of Panic Disorder

Recent psychiatric literature has suggested that panic disorder is associated with a biophysiologic abnormality, as demonstrated by the observed familial predisposition (Crowe 1984), the positive treatment response to specific pharmacologic agents (Sheehan 1982), and the specificity of response to provocative tests (lactate, CO_2, caffeine, clonidine, yohimbine, hyperventilation) (Hollander et al. 1988). This chapter reviews a cognitive model of anxiety, the neuroanatomic structures hypothesized to be involved in the genesis of anxiety and fear, and the information derived from studies of patients with panic disorder during their basal state and during a variety of provocative tests.

Although the brain structures and physiology involved in the sensations of anxiety and fear have not been entirely elucidated, a wealth of studies have greatly expanded current scientific knowledge. Both normal fear and abnormal anxiety responses involve specific deep brain structures more than the cerebral cortex (Marks 1987), specifically (1) the limbic system (hypothalamus, septum, hippocampus, amygdala, and cingulum); (2) other neuronal bodies including the thalamus, locus ceruleus, median raphe nuclei, and dental/interposital nuclei of the cerebellum; and (3) connections between these structures (Figure 4).

General Cognitive Model of Anxiety

Figure 5 depicts a model of anxiety derived from the work of Sarason (1982), Spielberger et al. (1971), and Schacter and Singer (1962). In this model, both genetic endowment and emotional experiences in childhood determine the degree to which a person scans the environment for threat and cognitively appraises stimuli for potential danger (Lader 1983). Much of this scanning and appraisal is unconscious, and the cognitive process and resultant anxiety may seem puzzling to the individual when the reasons for the behavior have been forgotten. When a threat is perceived, an arousal process occurs, which in turn heightens vigilance and prepares the body for appropriate action (the fight or flight response). Fear is experienced with similar concomitant physiologic changes, which are considered adaptive and biologically advantageous when the precipitating stimulus is actually threatening. When the stimulus is not

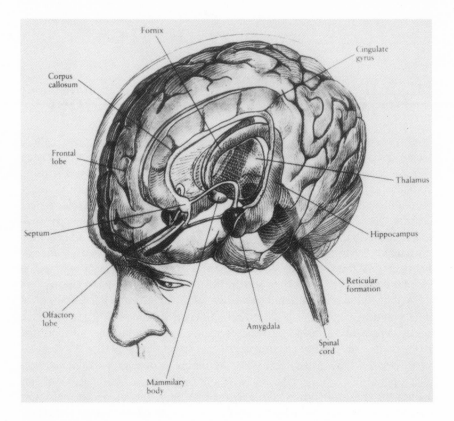

Figure 4.   Specific deep brain structures involved in fear and anxiety. Source: Bloom et al. *Brain, Mind, and Behavior*. 2d ed. Copyright 1985, 1988 by the Educational Broadcasting System. Reproduced with permission of W. H. Freeman and Co.

threatening or not apparent, however, the response is maladaptive.

Beck (1976) stated that pathologic anxiety arises from several errors in cognitive appraisal, including: overestimating the probability of a feared event; overestimating the severity of a feared event; underestimating coping resources (what can be done about it); and underestimating reserve factors (what others can do to help). Cognitive studies of patients with panic disorder have found that these patients display a marked tendency to overestimate and exaggerate dramatic consequences to their somatic symptoms of anxiety. Thus, rapid heartbeat induced by exercise, or sweating induced by a crowded, warm room may lead to thoughts of loss of control or even death. These thoughts provoke more anxiety, arousal, and somatic symptoms, and a vicious

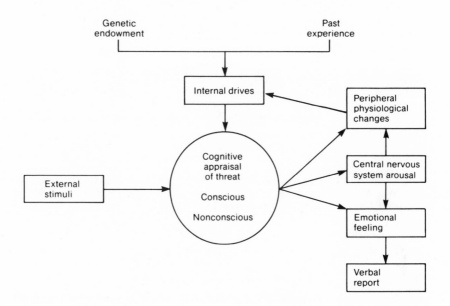

Figure 5. A general model of anxiety. Source: Adapted from Lader, M. Behavior and anxiety: Physiologic mechanisms. *Journal of Clinical Psychiatry* 44(11-Sec. 2):7, 1983. Copyright 1983 by Physicians Post-Graduate Press, Inc. Reproduced with permission.

cycle ensues (Rapee and Barlow 1988). Recently, the cognitive theory of panic has been used to explain nocturnal panic attacks whose occurrence had previously been used as evidence that panic disorder was a primarily biologic phenomenon (Roy-Byrne and Uhde 1988). Cognitive theorists have postulated that fluctuations in the internal physiologic state that occur during sleep may be sufficient to trigger anxiety and panic (Craske et al. 1989). Sleep of anxious patients has been characterized by a higher arousal level as shown by number of awakenings and changes in sleep stages. This cognitive model can be compared and contrasted to two prominent neurobiologic theories of anxiety: the septohippocampal theory and the locus ceruleus theory.

Septohippocampal Theory

Gray (1982) proposed a complex theory of the neurobiology of anxiety that implicates the hippocampus and its afferent and efferent connections. According to his hypothesis, the septohippocampal system is primarily responsible for integrating and responding to novel or unpleasant environmental cues (Figure 6). The major inputs, and hence those that produce anxiety, are signals that warn of punishment or nonreward, innate fear stimuli, and novel stimuli. The major outputs are inhibition of motor behavior, increased level of arousal, and

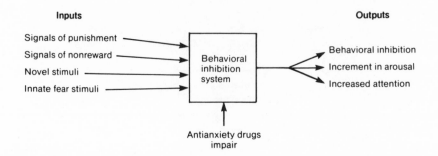

Figure 6.   Model of the behavioral inhibition system. Source: Adapted from Lader, M. Behavior and anxiety: Physiologic mechanisms. *Journal of Clinical Psychiatry* 44(11-Sec. 2):8, 1983. Copyright 1983 by Physicians Post-Graduate Press, Inc. Reproduced with permission.

increased attention to the environment, especially to novel elements.

Gray suggested that the septohippocampal system itself predicts the next sensory event to which the organism will be exposed, checks whether it actually does occur, and then inhibits behavior if there is a mismatch, or if the predicted event is aversive. Although the septohippocampal system does not store information, it has access to and may modify information from the temporal lobe.

Gray also attempted to neuroanatomically localize the inputs and outputs of the system. He postulated that the ascending norepinephrine projection to the septohippocampal system determines whether incoming stimuli are important; the ascending norepinephrine system to the hypothalamus primes the effector, autonomic, and motor systems for rapid action, if required; the ascending 5-HT projection adds information on whether this stimulus is associated with punishment; and the ascending cholinergic projection facilitates stimulus analysis. The prefrontal cortex and cingulate gyrus transmit to the septohippocampal system information for predicting sensory events and allow neocortical control of the septohippocampal system using verbally coded information.

Knowledge of this complex system is incomplete, but Gray's hypotheses have stimulated anxiety researchers to intensively study the involved neuroanatomical systems. The septohippocampal model clearly has many similarities to the cognitive model presented earlier, with the septohippocampal system acting as an ongoing appraiser of threat to the organism (Lader 1983).

Supportive research has demonstrated that electrical stimulation of the hippocampus, parahippocampal gyrus, and amygdala most commonly produce sensations of fear in awake human subjects (Gloor et al. 1982). Moreover, PET research has shown that patients who are vulnerable to lactate-induced panic attacks have abnormally low ratios of left-to-right parahippocampal blood flow, blood volume, and oxygen metabolism in the resting nonpanic state

(Reiman et al. 1986). Other researchers have found increased temporal lobe blood flow during panic in patients with panic disorder, as well as in controls with anticipatory anxiety (Curtis, unpublished paper). Research with the new MRI brain imaging technique (Fontaine et al. 1988) and brain electrical activity mapping (BEAM, a computerized spatial and temporal extension of conventional electroencephalography) (Abraham 1988) have also implicated temporal lobe abnormalities in panic disorder.

The Sympathetic Nervous System

Numerous studies have demonstrated that the sympathetic nervous system is critically important in responding to stimuli that threaten the well-being of an organism (Cannon 1953; Heninger and Charney 1988). Activation of the sympathetic nervous system increases both norepinephrine and epinephrine. This section reviews studies describing the central control mechanism (locus ceruleus) of the sympathetic nervous system as well as those measuring peripheral catecholamines in patients with panic disorder.

Locus Ceruleus Theory

The hippocampal formation receives abundant noradrenergic projections from the locus ceruleus (Price and Marall 1981; Charney et al. 1984). Figure 7 illustrates the presynaptic regulation of the locus ceruleus and lateral tegmental nuclei and their axonal projections innervating postsynaptic alpha-1, alpha-2, and β-adrenergic receptors (Charney et al. 1984).

The locus ceruleus (LC) is a tiny blue (cerulear) streak in the dorsolateral tegmentum of the pons, comprising only about 400 neurons. The locus ceruleus contains nearly half the noradrenergic neurons and produces more than 70 percent of the total noradrenaline found in the brain (Marks 1987). Activation of the locus ceruleus has been associated with fear and alarm reactions in monkeys (Redmond 1976). Bilateral lesions of the locus ceruleus in animals were associated with failure to show normal cardioaccelerator responses to threatening stimuli and lack of the associated behavioral response (Snyder et al. 1977).

The locus ceruleus has projections to many regions of the brain associated with responses of pain and fear, and also to the cerebral cortex, which is probably involved with the interpretation of the importance or relevance of stimuli as well as their cognitive associations (Svensson 1987). The locus ceruleus also projects to limbic areas, such as the amygdala, which are important for emotional and cardiovascular control.

Reiman and colleagues (1986) postulated, based on PET scan data, that a parahippocampal abnormality determines vulnerability to anxiety attacks. They further hypothesized that a triggering event, such as activation of the locus ceruleus projections to the hippocampal formation, causes the abnormal

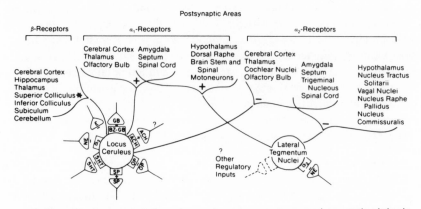

Schematized representation of complex neuroanatomy and neurophysiologic regulation of brain noradrenergic system. Presynaptic regulation of lucus ceruleus by a_2-adrenergic autoreceptors, and receptors for endogenous opiates, γ-aminobutyric acid, substance P, acetylcholine, serotonin, and epinephrine is illustrated. Specific projection patterns of locus ceruleus and lateral tegmentum nuclei are shown in relation to type of adrenergic postsynaptic receptor innervated. Brain areas listed are those containing moderate to high levels of receptor specified. a_2 indicates a_2-adrenergic autoreceptor; NE, norepinephrine; 5HT, serotonin; E, epinephrine; OP, opiate; ACH, acetylcholine; BZ-GB, benzodiazepine—γ-aminobutyric acid receptor complex; minus sign, inhibitory effect; plus sign, excitatory effect; asterisk, blocks frequency accommodation and enhances efficiency of sensory inputs.

Figure 7.   Brain noradrenergic function. Source: Charney et al. Noradrenergic function in panic anxiety. *Archives of General Psychiatry* 41(8):760, 1984. Copyright 1984 by the American Medical Association.

region to initiate an anxiety attack by way of the septoamygdalar complex and its sequential projections.

The locus ceruleus not only monitors external, novel stimuli and controls defensive behavioral and autonomic responses to these stimuli, but also monitors internal stimuli from organs innervated by the autonomic nervous system (Svensson 1987). Thus, the LC monitors the peripheral cardiovascular and respiratory state (Elam et al. 1984) as well as the function of the digestive and urogenital systems (Elam et al. 1986). This biologic integrative system alerts the individual to stimuli important to survival, whether the stimulus is a threatening external situation (e.g., getting robbed at gunpoint) or an internal visceral or cardiovascular stimulus (e.g., a gastrointestinal hemorrhage or hypotension).

The activity of the locus ceruleus is regulated by neuronal systems, including the alpha-2 adrenergic autoreceptor, benzodiazepine receptors, endogenous opiates, serotonin, norepinephrine, epinephrine, acetylcholine, gammaaminobutyric acid (GABA), and substance P (Charney et al. 1984). Charney and colleagues (1984) have studied the alpha-2 adrenergic receptor, which is a major regulator of noradrenergic activity. A major function of the brain noradrenergic system may be to enhance the effects of sensory information to specific brain sites (Charney and Heninger 1986). The alpha-2 adrenergic receptor is located presynaptically on neuronal cell bodies or terminals, and it regulates the release of norepinephrine through a negative feedback mechanism (Cedarbaum and Aghajanian 1977; Andrade and Aghajanian 1984).

Other neurotransmitters also have important effects on noradrenergic neural activity. Epinephrine, serotonin, opiates, GABA, and glycine decrease the locus ceruleus' rate of firing (Cedarbaum and Aghajanian 1977; Adrade and Aghajanian 1984; Segal 1979), while substance P, acetylcholine, and glutamate increase it (Guyenot and Aghajanian 1979). Drugs with anxiolytic effects such as benzodiazepines (Grant et al. 1983), tricyclic antidepressants (Svensson and Usdin 1978), morphine (Bird and Kuhar 1977), and the alpha-2 adrenergic agonist clonidine (Aghajanian 1978) depress locus ceruleus function, while drugs with anxiogenic effects, such as the alpha-2 adrenergic autoreceptor antagonist yohimbine, increase it (Holmberg and Gershon 1961; Charney et al. 1982).

The septohippocampal and locus ceruleus theories may be complementary or incompatible (Lader 1983). If the locus ceruleus functions to appraise external and internal stimuli, then it may be equivalent to the septohippocampal system in Gray's model.

Charney and colleagues (1984, 1986) studied the central control of the autonomic nervous system by carefully examining the status of the alpha-2 adrenergic system in patients with panic disorder and controls. They gave provocative challenges of drugs that are agonists, such as clonidine (since the alpha-2 adrenergic receptor is inhibitory, an agonist should cause decreased LC activity), as well as antagonists such as yohimbine (which should cause increased LC activity). Clonidine produced significantly greater decreases in plasma 3-methoxy-4-hydroxyphenylglycol (MHPG—a metabolite of norepinephrine) levels and sitting and standing blood pressure, and significantly less self-rated sedation in patients with panic disorder than in controls (Charney et al. 1986). Yohimbine caused significantly increased MHPG levels, blood pressure, and behavioral responses of anxiety in patients with panic disorder when compared with controls (Charney et al. 1984). This increased oscillatory range of noradrenergic activity, observed as an increased sensitivity to both clonidine (agonist) and yohimbine (antagonist), may indicate that patients with panic disorder have an abnormally regulated alpha-2 noradrenergic receptor system (Roy-Byrne and Cowley 1988).

In addition to central control of the autonomic nervous system, peripheral catecholamines have been extensively studied in research on anxiety and fear. Patients with panic disorder were found to have increased heart rate, skin conductance, electromyelogram activity, and skin temperature associated with most anxiety attacks (Freedman et al. 1985; Taylor et al. 1985; Roth et al. 1985; Shear 1986). Other researchers also found small increases in blood pressure, noradrenaline, plasma cortisol, and growth hormone during some attacks, but significant plasma epinephrine and MHPG changes were not observed (Cameron et al. 1987). Charney and colleagues (1984) found that MHPG was higher in patients with panic disorder who had frequent panic attacks than in normal controls or depressives.

At rest, panic disorder patients have tachycardia and heart rates that are more variable than controls (Taylor et al. 1985). Several investigators found increased plasma levels of epinephrine in the resting or basal state in patients with panic disorder (Villacres et al. 1987; Nesse et al. 1984; Appleby et al. 1981; Ballenger et al. 1984). Although early studies suggested plasma norepinephrine might also be elevated in anxious patients (Wyatt et al. 1971; Mathew et al. 1980; Ballenger et al. 1984), later studies found no such elevations (Villacres et al. 1987; Appleby et al. 1981; Carr et al. 1984; Nesse et al. 1984; Liebowitz et al. 1985).

Although the racing and pounding heartbeats, shortness of breath, sweating, rapid and deep breathing, and chest pain that typically occur during a panic attack suggest beta-adrenergic activation, as does the fact that tricyclic antidepressants, which are effective in treating panic disorder, down-regulate or decrease central beta-adrenergic receptor sensitivity (Charney et al. 1981a, b), recent evidence suggests that beta-adrenergic function may be decreased rather than increased in panic disorder (Nesse et al. 1984). Two studies of responses to infusions of isoproterenol (a beta-adrenergic agonist) have been carried out in patients with panic disorder (Nesse et al. 1984; Rainey et al. 1984). In one study, isoproterenol caused more panic attacks in patients with panic disorder than in controls, although the anxiety produced was less intense than with lactate infusion and no tachycardia occurred (Rainey et al. 1984a, b). In the second study, no increase in panic attacks was found in panic disorder patients, although the dosage of isoproterenol used was one-third of that in the first study (Nesse et al. 1984). The latter study actually showed decreased physiologic responsiveness to isoproterenol (decreased heart rates) in patients with panic disorder compared to controls. These two studies do not strongly support a beta-adrenergic abnormality in panic disorder. They are consistent with well-controlled studies showing that beta-blockers have only modest antianxiety effects and are not specifically effective in blocking panic attacks. For example, intravenously administered propranolol, in dosages sufficient to cause full beta-adrenergic blockade, is not able to block lactate-induced panic attacks in patients with panic disorder (Gorman et al. 1983).

Gamma-Aminobutyric Acid–Benzodiazepine Hypothesis

An exciting finding in anxiety research was the discovery of brain benzodiazepine (Bz) receptors (Insel et al. 1984). The Bz receptors are linked to a receptor for the inhibitory neurotransmitter GABA (Figure 8) (Skolnick and Paul 1983). Binding of a benzodiazepine to the Bz receptor facilitates the action of GABA, which is known to increase the permeability of chloride ions through the chloride ion channel. The heightened permeability of the cell to chloride ions decreases neuronal excitability by hyperpolarizing the neuronal membrane (Paul 1988). These diffuse, inhibitory short GABA-ergic circuits and associated Bz receptors are present throughout the brain and spinal cord. GABA and benzodiazepine have inhibitory effects on the locus ceruleus (Grant et al. 1980) and may also act to decrease anxiety by modulating the ascending activating systems (serotonergic, noradrenergic, and probably dopaminergic) that are implicated in the expression of fear (Marks and Tobena 1986).

There also appear to be endogenous anxiogenic compounds (betacarbolines and purines) that act on Bz receptors. Thus, these receptors may mediate both increases and decreases in anxiety (Roy-Byrne and Cowley 1988). Roy-Byrne and Veith (unpublished observations) found that panic patients may be less sensitive to the catecholamine-reducing effects of anxiolytic benzodiazepines. Woods, Charney, and Silver (1988*a*) reported that patients with panic disorder appear more sensitive to the effect of benzodiazepines with anxiogenic properties. Taken together, these results suggest that an abnormality of the Bz receptor may be present in patients with panic disorder.

Long-term alprazolam treatment of patients with panic disorder has been shown to reduce norepinephrine turnover, as evidenced by decreased baseline levels of the norepinephrine metabolite MHPG in plasma and the blunted yohimbine-induced increases in plasma MHPG, anxiety, and blood pressure

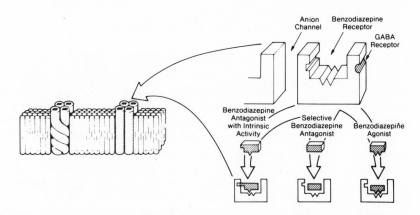

Figure 8. Model for GABA-receptor, benzodiazepine binding site, anion channel complex. Source: Insel et al. Benzodiazepine receptor-mediated model of anxiety. *Archives of General Psychiatry* 41(8):747, 1984. Copyright 1984 by the American Medical Association. Reproduced with permission.

(Charney and Heninger 1985). Other studies, however, suggested that alprazolam decreases the firing rate of the locus ceruleus only a small amount compared with imipramine or desipramine (Charney et al. 1981*a*). Gray (1977) postulated that rather than having their primary effect on noradrenergic systems, benzodiazepines enhance recurrent inhibition within the hippocampus (dampen input) or enhance feedback inhibition of both the septal and hippocampal systems.

Provocative Studies

Exhibit 10 lists the provocative laboratory studies carried out in recent years comparing patients with panic disorder and controls. These provocative tests enabled researchers to study in the laboratory the biophysiologic changes that occur during a panic attack and provided a conceptual framework for understanding complex phenomena (Uhde and Tancer 1988). Although the provocative tests fail to replicate all components of the panic attack, they have given researchers important information about the brain structures involved in these anxiety attacks.

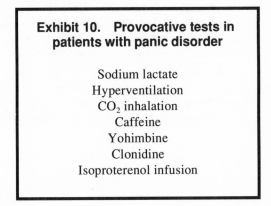

Exhibit 10.   Provocative tests in patients with panic disorder

Sodium lactate
Hyperventilation
CO_2 inhalation
Caffeine
Yohimbine
Clonidine
Isoproterenol infusion

Lactate Theory of Panic Disorder

Several researchers in the late 1940s and early 1950s found that patients with effort intolerance were distinguished from controls by their higher oxygen consumption with vigorous exercise and greater serum lactate production (Cohen and White 1950; Holmgren and Strom 1959; Jones and Mellerish 1946; Linko 1950). The increased serum lactate noted on exercise was hypothesized to be related to an increased muscle oxygen debt and a shift to an anaerobic metabolism (Ackerman and Sachar 1974).

This finding stimulated Pitts and McClure (1967) to speculate that patients with panic attacks were more sensitive to the effects of lactate than controls. They found that administration of 10 mg/kg of 0.5 molar sodium lactate infused over 20 minutes induced panic attacks in about 75 percent of patients with panic disorder and less than 5 percent of controls. This effect has now been replicated numerous times (Liebowitz et al. 1985; Cowley et al. 1987*a*; Rainey et al. 1984*b*; Margraf et al. 1986). Panic attacks are induced only in patients with panic disorder and not in patients with other psychiatric diagnoses (obsessive-compulsive disorder, major depression, social phobia, or bulimia) (Cowley et al. 1987*b*; Uhde and Tancer 1988). However, the interpretation of these findings in developing an overall theory of the genesis of panic attacks remains controversial (Margraf et al. 1986).

Several theories have been proposed to explain the association of sodium lactate infusion with panic attacks. The first suggests that sodium lactate produces nonspecific arousal and uncomfortable bodily sensations in all patients (both with and without panic disorder), but that the patients with panic disorder (owing to their hypervigilance) overreact to these sensations, as they do to many stimuli. Liebowitz and colleagues (1984) found that the higher the initial anxiety level, diastolic blood pressure, and heart rate of patients with panic disorder, the greater the likelihood of developing an anxiety attack with sodium lactate infusion. This suggests an interaction between the initial level of arousal, cognitive expectancy, and the effects of lactate (Margraf et al. 1986). Other evidence against lactate itself being a biochemical cause of panic is that moderate to strenuous exercise in normals frequently causes serum lactate to rise to levels similar to those resulting from lactate infusion without producing any anxiety (Ackerman and Sachar 1974).

Another theory suggests that the conversion of lactate to bicarbonate and CO_2 produces a transient intracerebral hypercapnia (causing stimulation of CO_2 brainstem chemoreceptors), since CO_2, but not bicarbonate, crosses the blood-brain barrier (Carr and Sheehan 1984). This theory is supported by the finding that patients with panic disorder are more sensitive to air with increased CO_2 concentrations than are controls (Gorman et al. 1986*c*).

Finally, Rainey and colleagues (1985) hypothesized that panic disorder results from a subtle defect in aerobic metabolism. This hypothesized defect explains the increased level of lactate seen with exercise, the increase in oxygen consumption and lactate levels in patients with panic disorder versus controls who are infused with lactate, and the panic response to a variety of other challenges (yohimbine, caffeine, and CO_2) that increase metabolic demand.

The two main physiologic differences consistently found in patients with lactate-induced panic are hyperventilation and tachycardia (Liebowitz et al. 1985). Both metabolic and respiratory alkalosis develop in all subjects during lactate infusion, but only hyperventilation-induced hypocapnia differentiates patients at the point of lactate-induced panic from nonpanicking patients and normal controls (Liebowitz et al. 1985). Low inorganic phosphate levels at baseline also appear associated with patients who panic during lactate infusion

(Gorman et al. 1986a). Other than this, few consistent biochemical changes differentiate patients who panic during lactate infusion and controls who do not (Carr et al. 1986).

Researchers have demonstrated that when panic disorder patients are successfully treated with either imipramine or alprazolam and then retested with lactate infusion, most patients no longer develop panic attacks. This suggests a protective biologic change induced by medication in these patients (Roy-Byrne and Cowley 1988).

Carbon Dioxide Hypersensitivity

Studies of patients with soldier's heart suggested that these patients displayed intolerable hyperpnea at lower levels of CO_2 than normals (Drury 1987). In the 1950s, patients with neurocirculatory asthenia (a syndrome that is also virtually indistinguishable from panic disorder) were found to have a greater increase in ventilation in response to muscular work than normals and were more likely to have anxiety attacks with 4-percent CO_2 than were controls (Cohen and White 1950). Patients with hyperventilation syndrome have also been reported to have abnormalities in the CO_2 ventilatory response to carbon dioxide inhalation (Folgering and Colla 1978).

Several studies have now demonstrated that a significantly higher number of patients with panic disorder than controls have anxiety attacks with 5-percent carbon dioxide inhalation (Gorman et al. 1984, 1986c; Woods et al. 1988b; Gorman et al. 1988a). Room air contains virtually no CO_2 (0.5 percent). Five-percent CO_2 in room air will triple minute ventilation in most normal subjects (Mitchell et al. 1963), and concentrations of CO_2 over 12 percent induce central nervous system and respiratory depression (Berger et al. 1977). Woods and colleagues (1988b) found that, although the frequency of panic attacks and the increases in anxiety and somatic symptoms induced by 5-percent CO_2 were greater in panic attack patients than in controls, 7.5-percent CO_2 induced quite similar severe anxiety and somatic symptoms in the healthy controls.

Panic with CO_2 has been associated with an exaggerated ventilatory response and increases in plasma norepinephrine and diastolic blood pressure (Gorman et al. 1988a). Gorman postulated that patients with panic disorder may have hypersensitive CO_2 receptors or CO_2 receptors with low setpoints. When triggered by increasing CO_2, these receptors evoke a subjective panic associated with an exaggerated ventilatory response and consequent hypocapnic alkalosis. Patients may "learn" to hyperventilate to maintain low levels of CO_2 and avoid triggering their CO_2 sensors; this would explain the previous finding that patients with panic disorder are chronic hyperventilators (Liebowitz et al. 1985).

Alternatively, increasing CO_2 may cause panic by stimulating the locus ceruleus (Woods et al. 1985, 1988*b*; Redmond 1979). Carbon dioxide increases brain catecholamine synthesis (Carlsson et al. 1977; Garcia de Yebenes Prous et al. 1977) and norepinephrine turnover (Garcia de Yebenes Prous et al. 1977) in the rat, increases the firing rate of neurons in the rat noradrenergic locus ceruleus (Elam et al. 1981), and increases the plasma levels of the norepinephrine metabolite MHPG in the rhesus monkey. Also, lesions in the locus ceruleus have reduced by 30 to 80 percent the CO_2-induced increase in brain biogenic amine release (Oke et al. 1983).

A final hypothesis states that, while breathing increased CO_2 causes increased somatic symptoms in all persons, the hypervigilance (increased alertness to subtle changes in their physiologic status) and tendency to cognitively catastrophize of patients with panic disorder leads to a conditioned hyperresponse (Clark 1986*a*; Evans 1972). This is supported by a recent study of patients with panic disorder that demonstrated that having an illusion that they could control the amount of carbon dioxide they were administered led to a reduction in the number of DSM-III-R panic attack symptoms, a rating of less intense symptoms, a report of less subjective anxiety attacks and catastrophic cognitions, and significantly less anxiety when exposed to CO_2 compared to subjects without an illusion of control (Sanderson et al. 1989).

Caffeine Provocation of Anxiety

Caffeine is a xanthine derivative and is a widely used psychotropic agent in North America, with daily consumption averaging 200 to 250 mg per adult (Gilbert 1981). In short-term administration, caffeine increases alertness, stimulates attention, and helps restore performance that is decreased by factors such as boredom and fatigue (Boulenger et al. 1984; Weiss and Laties 1962). Caffeine can, in doses above 600 mg/day, induce a syndrome of caffeinism. It is characterized by nervousness, anxiety, sleep disturbance, and psychophysiologic symptoms (rapid heartbeat, chest tightness, dyspnea) that may be indistinguishable from panic disorder (Greden 1974).

Several researchers have found that patients with panic disorder consume less caffeine than normal control subjects or patients with major depression, presumably because of its anxiogenic effect (Boulenger et al. 1984; Lee et al. 1988). Greater sensitivity to caffeine among panic disorder patients has been shown by direct caffeine challenge (Charney et al. 1985; Uhde et al. 1985*b*). Charney and colleagues (1985) also demonstrated that caffeine (10mg/kg) produced significantly greater increases in subject-rated anxiety, nervousness, fear, nausea, palpitations, restlessness, and tremors in patients with panic disorder compared to healthy controls. These effects in panic disorder patients were significantly correlated with plasma caffeine levels, and almost three-quarters of the panic disorder patients reported that the behavioral effects of caffeine were similar to those experienced during panic attacks. Caffeine did not alter MHPG levels in patients or controls and increased plasma cortisol equally in these two groups. Following caffeine challenge, panic patients had higher plasma lactate levels than did controls, suggesting that caffeine does have a metabolic stimulating effect and may have a mechanism of action similar to lactate.

Several mechanisms of action for caffeine have been proposed, including inhibition of phosphodiesterase (Butcher and Sutherland 1962), antagonism of benzodiazepine (Marangos et al. 1979) and adenosine receptor function (Snyder and Sklar 1984), and increased brain catecholamine activity (Berkowitz et al. 1970). The inhibition of adenosine receptor function is currently favored as the mechanism for caffeine-induced anxiety and stimulation (Snyder and Sklar 1984; Charney et al. 1985), because the brain concentration of caffeine required to block adenosine receptors is within the range seen following normal doses of caffeine.

There is considerable evidence that adenosine and other purines act as neuromodulators with important regulatory effects on multiple neuronal systems throughout the brain (Charney et al. 1985; Stone 1981; Patel et al. 1982). Adenosine potently *inhibits* the release of acetylcholine (Ginsborg and Hirst 1972) and norepinephrine (Enero and Saidman 1977) centrally, and caffeine antagonizes the effects of adenosine on neurotransmitter release and causes increased norepinephrine and acetylcholine release (Stone 1981). Adenosine has been shown by electrophysiologic studies to reduce the spontaneous firing rate of neurons in the cerebral cortex, cerebellum, and locus ceruleus (Olpe et al. 1983). These inhibitory effects of adenosine occur via interactions with adenosine receptors and are blocked by caffeine (Charney et al. 1985). Thus, caffeine and other methylxanthines, such as theophylline and isobutylmethylxanthine, increase the firing of cortical neurons and the locus ceruleus and may produce their stimulatory effects by this mechanism.

Summary of Psychobiologic Studies

The plethora of provocative tests of panic disorder, the research on brain receptors, and the recent MRI, PET scan, and BEAM studies have produced an exponential growth of knowledge on the psychobiology of panic disorder and other types of anxiety. However, the complexity of the brain has thus far prevented the full elucidation of brain mechanisms involved in anxiety. As in many other medical illnesses, treatment has preceded full understanding of pathophysiology. Also, analogous to medical illnesses such as peptic ulcer disease, knowledge of factors that provoke a relapse of symptoms (such as alcohol, spicy foods, or coffee in peptic ulcer disease) does not necessarily clarify the pathophysiologic mechanisms in that disease. Future biologic research promises not only to unravel the enigma of pathologic anxiety, but also to add to our knowledge of overall brain physiologic function.

Chapter 10

Treatment of Panic Disorder

The key principles of panic disorder treatment reviewed in this section include the following:

- Negotiation of explanatory models of illness between patient and physician
- Pharmacologic blockade of the panic attacks
- Psychotherapy aimed at specific social problems (marital problems, family dysfunction) and/or psychologic vulnerabilities (poor self-esteem, rejection sensitivity)
- Behaviorally oriented treatment to deal with phobic-avoidant behavior left after pharmacologic treatment
- Education about relapse and recurrence of symptoms

Because the most frightening aspects of panic disorder are the somatic symptoms and the cultural stigma of mental illness, many patients with panic attacks believe they have a severe physical illness (Katon 1984). The first stage in the treatment of panic disorder in primary care is to negotiate explanatory models of illness with the patient (Katon and Kleinman 1980). To elicit patients' beliefs about their illness, Kleinman and colleagues (1978) recommended initially asking them several open-ended questions about their view of the illness:

- What does the patient believe is wrong?
- What type and style of treatment does the patient expect?
- What outcomes would be considered as effective care?

If these do not elicit the necessary information, then the physician should inquire specifically about the patient's beliefs concerning each of five issues:

- Cause of the illness
- Reasons for the onset of symptoms at a particular time
- Pathophysiology
- Course (severity and type of sickness role)
- Treatment

To elicit such information, physicians must demonstrate warmth, empathy, and persistence, and they must be nonjudgmental. Most of all, physicians must have a genuine interest in the meaning the sickness has for the patients and must make explicit to the patients their intent to draw on this essential information in constructing an appropriate treatment plan.

Patients with panic disorder are often convinced that they have a cardiac or neurologic disorder and that their anxiety or nervousness is secondary to their physical symptoms. Studies that support this patient perception have shown that, during a panic attack, fear and anxiety are late symptoms following autonomic symptoms such as dyspnea, palpitations, chest pain, and hot or cold flashes (Katerdnahl 1988). Indeed, evidence suggests that generalized anxiety and avoidance behavior usually follow the onset of panic attacks, rather than preceding the severe episodic anxiety (Uhde et al. 1985).

When the physician tells patients with panic attacks that they have a severe anxiety disorder, they often feel that the physician does not believe that they have "real" physical symptoms (Katon 1986). It is very helpful to educate these patients about the biologic research on panic disorder. Explaining that panic disorder results from a dysfunction of the sympathetic nervous system, in which bursts of catecholamines are released into the peripheral circulation causing symptoms such as tachycardia, chest pain, dyspnea, and dizziness, often decreases patient defensiveness. A further analogy about panic attacks being quite similar to the fight-or-flight response may help. Thus, the patient is provided with the following explanation: "If you were walking down a dark street and heard a sudden sound, your heart might begin to race, your respiratory rate might increase, you would feel tense, shaky, warm, sweaty, and you would be prepared to either flee or fight for your life. These attacks you are having are set off by dysregulation of the same area of the brain that controls the fight-or-flight response, but you are having this alarm or danger response at inappropriate times when there is no actual danger." This explanation also leads naturally to a discussion of the effectiveness of medications that dampen psychophysiologic activation of the autonomic nervous system.

Patients often describe the anxiety attacks by emphasizing that since their episodes began, stresses that they frequently coped with quite well now lead to symptoms, and that such attacks occur regardless of whether they are anxious or stressed by life circumstances. Here the physician can emphasize that panic disorder causes the alarm mechanisms in the brain to be hypersensitive (the phenomenon of sensitization) to any stresses the patient faces (Weekes 1976) and, in addition, will often discharge with no apparent stress present. Not only is the patient's autonomic nervous system sensitized to external stresses, but minor physiologic symptoms such as rapid heart rate or sweating induced by exercise may also provoke an alarm response.

The physician must also recognize that many patients are quite demoralized about their symptoms, and it is important to project an image of confidence in the diagnosis. Patients should be told that this is a common disorder afflicting an estimated 5 million Americans and that the physician has treated many cases effectively. A lack of fear of the symptoms on the physician's part, a thorough but reasonable and brief medical workup, and the willingness to tolerate a fairly large amount of dependency in the first few days, weeks, and occasionally months of this problem are all essential and desirable physician behaviors.

Psychopharmacologic Treatment

Recent double-blind, placebo-controlled studies have demonstrated that three classes of medications are effective for the treatment of panic disorder:

1. Tricyclic antidepressants
2. Monoamine oxidase inhibitors
3. High-potency benzodiazepines

Preliminary results of a multinational study have demonstrated that imipramine, phenelzine, and alprazolam are all more effective than placebo in the treatment of panic disorder, and the three medications do not differ significantly in efficacy (Sheehan et al. 1980, 1984). The physician should become familiar with one or two medications from each of these classes.

The goal of psychopharmacologic treatment is to block spontaneous panic attacks (Roy-Byrne et al. in press). Avoidance behavior and social phobias often develop secondary to these spontaneous attacks and, after pharmacologic blockade of the anxiety attacks is achieved, it is important to push patients to reexpose themselves to these phobic situations.

This advice is helpful in two ways. First, it helps determine whether complete pharmacologic blockade of the panic attacks has been achieved. If the patient still breaks through with occasional panic attacks, the dosage of medication should be increased until the patient has no further acute panic attacks. Emphasize to patients that they can and will still have generalized or free-floating anxiety and nervousness and anxiety in stressful situations, but they should not have the severe bursts of autonomic symptoms (tachycardia, dyspnea, chest pain, diaphoresis, dizziness).

The second main reason for patients to reexpose themselves to phobic situations is to reexperience the situation and realize that they no longer need to avoid it because their anxiety attacks have gone away. This knowledge frequently markedly decreases avoidance behavior, phobias, and anticipatory anxiety.

Make it clear to patients that they may have to enter phobic situations without having anxiety attacks several times before their anticipatory anxiety decreases. In some cases, the patient is remarkably recalcitrant to enter feared or phobic situations, and the addition of behavioral psychotherapeutic techniques may be necessary.

Patients with panic disorder are one of the most difficult groups of patients to treat with medications. All psychopharmacologic treatments have side effects, and these patients are already hypervigilant about bodily symptoms. Patients with panic disorder also have a strong sense of feeling out of control due to the dysregulation of their autonomic nervous system, and they are often desperately trying to control their lives by increasing exercise, constricting their social contacts to a minimum, and at times, using alcohol or sedative-hypnotic agents. The idea of taking a medication that will have central nervous system therapeutic and side effects frequently makes them feel even more out of control and frightened. These patients often take the prescribed medication for a few days and then stop, reporting that it causes symptoms like jitteriness, nervousness, and tachycardia—the very symptoms they presented initially. Several useful treatment strategies to increase compliance include the following:

1. Advise all patients that they may have side effects from the medications, and list the common ones. If they can tolerate 1 or 2 weeks of side effects, the anxiety attacks can be cured. Thus, the temporary discomfort of the psychopharmacologic side effects is reframed as evidence that the medicine is working and as a challenge they need to cope with to attain effective treatment.
2. See these patients at least once a week and be available by telephone to answer questions about side effects. Emphasize to the patients that they should *never* stop the medication without calling first to get the doctor's advice, or time will be wasted until their next appointment. Few patients actually call, but many report afterwards that the security of knowing they could have called decreased their anxiety.
3. Continue increasing the medication dosage until the patient is entirely free of acute panic attacks. A common mistake in primary care is to partially alleviate symptoms, but stop short of full dosage and amelioration of anxiety attacks.
4. Give patients lay books or articles to read about panic attacks. This information is helpful, reassuring, and enables the patient to feel more in control (see suggested readings).
5. Describe the approximate dosage of medication that the patients will need to alleviate their panic attacks (e.g., 150 to 300 mg of a tricyclic antidepressant), but give the patient as much control as possible over how fast the dosage is increased.

Tricyclic Antidepressants

In primary care medicine, the usual first pharmacologic treatment for panic disorder should be the tricyclic antidepressants. These medications are quite safe, and they are the most extensively studied medications in the treatment of panic disorder (Katon 1986). In addition, studies of primary care patients with panic disorder have found that about 50 percent of these patients have a concurrent major depression, and tricyclic antidepressants work effectively in the treatment of both disorders.

The best studied tricyclic antidepressant in the treatment of panic disorder is imipramine (Sheehan et al. 1980; Klein 1964; Zitrin 1983). Nine of ten double-blind placebo-controlled studies have found it to be significantly more effective than placebo (Roy-Byrne and Katon 1987). Uncontrolled studies have shown that desipramine, nortriptyline, amitriptyline, clomipramine (not yet released in the United States), and doxepin are also effective agents (Liebowitz et al. 1986; Gloger et al. 1981; Roy-Byrne et al. in press; Lydiard 1988).

Other antidepressant medications are either untested or have had negative results in patients with panic disorder. Trazodone and maprotiline have been found to be of questionable value in the treatment of panic disorder (Lydiard 1988). Fluoxetine has not yet been tested in panic disorder, and amoxapine should be reserved for patients with psychotic symptoms (it is metabolized in the body to an antipsychotic and antidepressant). A useful strategy is to start the patient on a low dose, such as 25 mg of imipramine or desipramine, and to gradually increase it by 25 mg every 3 days. It helps to tell the patient that you would like to gradually increase the medication to 150 mg to 300 mg or until the panic attacks totally cease. Give the patient the every-3-day increase schedule, but also suggest that if problematic side effects occur, they can slow down the rate of increase.

About 1 in 10 people get an excitatory or stimulant-like effect with imipramine or desipramine. Tell patients that if this occurs, they may have started at too high a dosage. Then decrease the dosage to 10 mg of imipramine or desipramine and increase it by 10 mg increments every 3 days. If the patient still has stimulatory effects, change to a less noradrenergic drug, such as 25 mg of nortriptyline. An alternate strategy is to temporarily add a low dose of alprazolam—0.5 mg two or three times a day—to the tricyclic. This decreases the stimulatory side effect and allows a gradual increase in the tricyclic antidepressant dosage. For those rare patients who cannot tolerate this side effect, switch to a monoamine oxidase inhibitor or benzodiazepine.

Table 2 lists the tricyclic antidepressants and their common side effects (Katon and Roy-Byrne 1988). All available tricyclics have some degree of anticholinergic action; the possible side effects include dry mouth, constipation, blurry vision, urinary retention, sinus tachycardia, and memory dysfunction (Frazer and Conway 1974). Should a serious anticholinergic effect occur, switch to a tricyclic with a low anticholinergic agent such as desipramine. Sedation can also be a problem, especially with amitriptyline, doxepin, trimipramine, and trazodone. Should this occur, switching to a nonsedating tricyclic such as desipramine is often helpful. Other less common adverse effects of the antidepressants are weight gain and sexual dysfunction. Fluoxe-

Table 2. Pharmacologic properties of the polycyclic antidepressants

| | Potency of reuptake blockade | | Dosage (mg) | Histamine$_1$ | Anticholinergic | Sedation | Orthostatic hypotension |
	Serotonin	Norepi-nephrine					
Tertiary amines							
Doxepin (Sinequan)	***	**	100-300	Highest	Moderate	High	***
Amitriptyline (Elavil)	****	**	100-300	Mod-Hi	Highest	High	***
Imipramine (Tofranil)	****	**	100-300	Low	Moderate	Moderate	**
Trimipramine (Surmontil)	*	*	100-300	High	Moderate	High	***
Secondary amines							
Nortriptyline (Pamelor)	***	***	50-125	Low	Low	Moderate	*
Protriptyline (Vivactil)	***	****	20-60	Low	High	Low	*
Desipramine (Norpramin)	**	****	100-300	Low	Low	Low	*
Amoxapine (Ascendin)	**	***	100-300	?	Low	Low	**
Tetracyclic							
Maprotiline (Ludiomil)	*	***	100-300	Moderate	Low	Moderate	**
Trazolopyridine							
Trazodone (Desyrel)	***	*	150-500	Low	Lowest	High	***
Bicyclic							
Fluoxetine (Prozac)	****	0	20-80	?	Lowest	Low	0

Source: Katon and Roy-Byrne 1988.
0 = None, * = Slight, ** = Moderate, *** = Marked, **** = Pronounced

tine appears to have less propensity to cause weight gain, but it is currently untested in panic disorder (Wernicke 1985).

All tricyclics have significant effects on the heart (Bigger et al. 1978). They tend to slow both atrial and ventricular depolarization and cause an increase in PR, QRS, and QT intervals as well as a decrease in T-wave amplitude. The tricyclics all have quinidine-like effects on the heart, slowing conduction time through the bundle of His (Bigger et al. 1978). The tricyclics, like other Group I antiarrhythmics, can cause abnormally slow post-AV nodal conduction. Many patients with anxiety attacks complain of irregular heartbeats and are found to have premature ventricular contractions. It is not surprising that tricyclic therapy often strikingly decreases their ventricular irritability; ventricular ectopia is not a contraindication to tricyclic use (Bigger et al. 1977).

Because tricyclics cause slowing of conduction time through the bundle of His, the physician should be most cautious with panic disorder patients who have preexisting bundle-branch blocks on EKG (Bigger et al. 1978). In these patients, treatment should proceed cautiously with an initial 25 mg dosage of a tricyclic and increases of 25 mg every 5 to 7 days. These patients should be followed with serial electrocardiograms.

Several studies have found that tricyclic antidepressants do not decrease myocardial contractility in therapeutic dosages. Veith and colleagues (1982) used radionucleotide ventriculography to measure ventricular ejection fractions before and during maximum exercise in depressed patients who had heart disease and were being treated with therapeutic dosages of doxepin and imipramine. No adverse effects on left ventricular function were noted. Another study in a group of 21 depressed patients with left ventricular impairment found that ejection fraction was unchanged by nortriptyline (Roose et al. 1986).

The most common side effect that limits tricyclic dosage is orthostatic hypotension (Katon and Roy-Byrne 1988). Although tricyclic-induced orthostatic hypotension had been thought to be due to alpha-1 adrenergic blockade, the relative hypotensive effects of specific tricyclic drugs do not follow the alpha-1 receptor blocking pattern. A number of factors are associated with an increased likelihood of orthostatic hypotension, including:

1. The concomitant use of one or more medications that can lower blood pressure (antihypertensive agents, diuretics, and sedative-hypnotics are the most common offenders) (Tesar et al. 1987*a*).
2. The type of antidepressant used (Frazer and Conway 1974).
3. The presence of cardiovascular disease (Glassman et al. 1983).
4. The presence of a pretreatment postural systolic blood pressure drop of greater than 10 mm Hg (Glassman et al. 1979). In the elderly, conditions such as diabetes, peripheral neuropathy, cardiovascular

and cerebrovascular disease, varicose veins, electrolyte imbalance, and idiopathic orthostasis largely account for the increased prevalence of orthostatic hypotension.

5. Dietary avoidance of salt by patients with medical illnesses such as hypertension and cardiac disease.

The following guidelines are especially useful in medically ill geriatric patients to minimize serious sequelae secondary to orthostatic hypotension (Halaris et al. 1986-87).

1. Take baseline orthostatic blood pressure on medically ill and geriatric patients and evaluate patients thoroughly for the presence of medical conditions predisposing to orthostasis, including idiopathic orthostasis.

2. Reduce, when possible, the dosage of nonpsychotropic agents with a propensity to induce orthostasis, before a second drug is added to the regimen.

3. Tricyclic antidepressants should be started in very low dosages and increased gradually while monitoring orthostatic changes. If orthostatic changes occur, dividing the dosage throughout the day is very helpful.

4. Advise the patient to use salt and at times to even add salt substitutes to the diet (when not contraindicated by serious medical illness).

5. Monitor, if possible, blood pressure and pulse daily in the supine and erect positions. This is particularly important during the first week of treatment and after dosage adjustments.

6. Instruct the patient not to rise abruptly from the lying or sitting position.

7. Prescribe surgical elastic stockings during the first few weeks of treatment to prevent blood pooling in the extremities. Abdominal binders have been reported to be effective in intractable cases, as is the occasional addition of a stimulant (e.g., methylphenidate).

8. Use nortriptyline, which may have a decreased potential to cause orthostatic hypotension compared to other tricyclics, in high-risk patients. Roose and colleagues (1986) found that only 5 percent of nortriptyline-treated elderly patients with cardiac constrictive disease and congestive heart failure developed orthostatic hypotension compared to 42 percent who were treated with imipramine.

Therapeutic monitoring of blood levels of tricyclics should be reserved for nonresponsive patients (Roy-Byrne et al. in press). Dosages of the traditional tricyclics (with the exception of nortriptyline and protriptyline) should be increased gradually until panic attacks have stopped. If 300 mg is reached and the patient still has anxiety attacks, a serum level 12 hours after the last dose should be drawn. If the serum level is below the therapeutic range, the dosage should be increased in 25- to 50-mg increments. Other reasons to draw a blood level include moderate to severe side effects and suspicion of noncompliance.

There is a large variability in blood levels of tricyclics, probably due to differences in absorption and metabolism of the drug (Halaris 1986). This is especially true in the elderly. Thus, serious side effects may suggest that serum levels are higher than needed, and lowering the dosage may enhance response and decrease side effects. Nortriptyline has a therapeutic window of 50 to 150 ng/ml, and serum levels below or above usually do not provide a therapeutic response for depression (Amsterdam et al. 1980).

The clinical implications of blood levels of imipramine and desipramine have been relatively well established and suggest a sigmoidal dose relationship. Preliminary studies in patients with panic disorder suggest that for imipramine, a serum level above 150 ng/ml is most effective, and for desipramine, a serum level above 125 ng/ml appears to be most effective (Lydiard 1988). Research is in progress to further delineate effective serum levels in the treatment of panic disorder.

The mechanism of action of the tricyclic antidepressants in panic disorder is unclear. The catecholamine theory of depression suggested a depletion of catecholamines, norepinephrine, and serotonin, and, therefore, a decrease in synaptic transmission in areas of the brain that control affective regulation (limbic system) (Schildkraut 1965). According to this theory, tricyclic antidepressants prevent neurotransmitters in the neurosynaptic cleft from being re-

---

Successful Treatment of Panic Disorder With a Tricyclic Antidepressant

Mr. O was a 35-year-old engineer who presented with symptoms of headache, dizziness, rapid heart rate, dyspnea, and paresthesias 3 weeks after a severe auto accident. A careful neurologic workup including physical examination, skull x rays, and CT scan proved negative. After Mr. O described increased nervousness and social phobic behavior (inability to be comfortable in meetings and conferences at work), his family physician referred him for psychiatric consultation. He was diagnosed as having panic disorder and started on imipramine 25 mg. Mr. O telephoned 3 days later and reported feeling "speeded up" on the medication as if he had drunk too much coffee. He was advised to continue imipramine, but at the lower dosage of 10 mg. This decreased the sense of feeling "speeded up." The medication was then gradually increased to 150 mg over 3 to 4 weeks, with complete amelioration of panic attacks. His social phobic behavior also rapidly disappeared, and he continued to go to meetings, finding he was no longer having anxiety attacks.

turned to the sending neuron, and thus more of these chemicals are available for synaptic transmission. However, maximal reuptake blockade occurs in the first week of treatment, whereas maximum therapeutic effects occur in the second and third weeks (Charney et al. 1981b). Some evidence suggests that therapeutic efficacy results from changes tricyclics induce in the sensitivities of neurotransmitter receptors, whose time course correlates better with the onset of clinical improvement (Charney et al. 1981b). Imipramine has been shown to decrease the sensitivity of beta-adrenergic receptors and to decrease locus ceruleus activity in animals (Charney et al. 1981a). Imipramine also decreases plasma MHPG (a marker of central norepinephrine turnover), and this reduction is associated with a decrease in the signs and symptoms of panic attacks (Charney et al. 1984; Charney and Heninger 1986).

Benzodiazepines

The introduction of the high-potency benzodiazepine, alprazolam, has altered the perception that benzodiazepines are not effective in panic disorder. Alprazolam has been found to be as effective as imipramine and phenelzine in the treatment of panic disorder (Sheehan 1983; Sheehan et al. 1984; Ballenger et al. 1988). Two other high-potency benzodiazepines, clonazepam and lorazepam, also appear to be effective antipanic drugs (Charney et al. 1987; Tesar et al. 1987b). Moreover, a study of high-dosage diazepam (a mean of 30 mg/day) has found that it also markedly decreases panic attacks, suggesting that older studies may have suffered from too low a dosage as well as infrequent dosing (Dunner et al. 1986).

The benzodiazepines' therapeutic efficacy appears to be secondary to their ability to facilitate inhibitory neurotransmission via potentiation of the action of GABA (Insel et al. 1984; Skolnick and Paul 1983). Benzodiazepines bind stereo-specifically to receptors linked to GABA, which have their highest density in limbic brain areas controlling affective arousal and autonomic function. Also, benzodiazepine-GABA receptors are in the area of the locus ceruleus that inhibits the neuronal activity of this modulator of the autonomic nervous system (Marks and Tobena 1986).

Alprazolam and lorazepam have relatively short plasma half-lives (Table 3) and, thus, require three to four daily dosages, whereas clonazepam and diazepam have relatively long half-lives usually requiring only two daily dosages. The advantages of benzodiazepines in the treatment of panic disorder are that they have a rapid onset of action and are well tolerated with few side effects. However, several disadvantages tend to deter the clinician from their use as a first-line antipanic drug (Roy-Byrne et al. in press). These disadvantages include:

1. As many as 50 percent of patients with panic disorder have a concurrent major depression and, with the possible exception of alprazolam,

Table 3.   Classification of benzodiazepines by plasma half-life

Generic	Brand	Half-life (hours)
Very short		
Triazolam	Halcion	2–6
Short		
Alprazolam	Xanax	6–20
Lorazepam	Ativan	9–22
Oxazepam	Serax	6–24
Temazepam	Restoril	5–20
Intermediate		
Chlordiazepoxide	Librium	7–46
Diazepam	Valium	14–90
Clonazepam	Klonopin	20–40
Long		
Clorazepate	Tranxene	30–200
Halazepam	Paxipam	30–200
Prazepam	Verstran	30–200
Very long		
Flurazepam	Dalmane	90–200

benzodiazepines are not effective antidepressants.

2. Although the potential for abuse is low, this can be a problem if patients who have a propensity to abuse drugs are not excluded.
3. The benzodiazepines are more difficult to taper than are tricyclic antidepressants or monoamine oxidase inhibitors (Fyer et al. 1987).

Because of the above concerns, benzodiazepines should be reserved for patients with panic disorder who do not tolerate tricyclic antidepressants and who elect not to try monoamine oxidase inhibitors owing to concerns over the potential "cheese reaction" (see below). Another use of these agents is to prescribe them concurrently with a tricyclic in the first few weeks of therapy to try to decrease anxiety and the tendency to worry about antidepressant side effects. The benzodiazepines may also help decrease the initial stimulatory tricyclic effects. Despite the admonitions against their use in primary care as a first-line drug, the benzodiazepines are effective in panic disorder, and they are useful medications for those patients who do not tolerate tricyclics.

Several types of patients should not be treated with benzodiazepines because of their likelihood to abuse them. Marks (1983) has shown that the majority of patients who abuse benzodiazepines have a history of polydrug or

Successful Treatment of Panic Disorder
With a Benzodiazepine

Mrs. A was a 43-year-old married white management banker. She presented to her primary physician with long-term anxiety problems. Mrs. A described acute attacks of rapid heartbeat, dyspnea, sweating, tremulousness, and nausea for more than 10 years. She avoided most social situations because of these attacks, and her activities were limited to driving to work and back and spending time with her husband. She had recently received a promotion that would require taking clients to lunch and taking training seminars, and she was quite afraid she could not cope with these increased responsibilities with her social phobias. Mrs. A had taken diazepam intermittently for 10 years, but it had not stopped her acute anxiety attacks.

Mrs. A was initially tried on three different tricyclic antidepressants, but reported all caused side effects such as sedation, a "spacey" feeling, and constipation. She was then started on alprazolam 0.25 mg PO TID, which was increased to 0.5 mg PO TID over 2 weeks with a rapid cessation in panic attacks. Her primary care physician worked with Mrs. A to add several new social activities a month, and she was delighted to find she no longer experienced anxiety attacks. She accepted her promotion, was successful in taking several seminars, and began to actually enjoy going to lunch with colleagues and clients. She has remained asymptomatic for the last 2 years on alprazolam 0.5 mg PO TID.

alcohol abuse. Thus, a history of polydrug or alcohol abuse should be a contraindication to the use of these agents. Patients with personality disorders and chronic benign pain conditions (back pain, headaches) also should not be treated with benzodiazepines. Finally, patients with first-degree relatives who abuse alcohol may be at increased risk for abuse of benzodiazepines. Thus, a complete individual psychiatric and family history is necessary before these agents are prescribed.

Benzodiazepines are well absorbed on an empty stomach and are oxidized by microsomal enzymes in the liver to active metabolites, which in turn are conjugated in the liver and excreted in the urine (Roy-Byrne et al. in press). The main side effects of benzodiazepines are sedation and psychomotor impairment (Greenblatt and Shader 1974). Fatigue, ataxia, slurred speech, and amnesia can also occur. Sedation often appears in the first few days of treatment and tends to decrease in 1 to 2 weeks. Psychomotor impairment as well as effects on recent memory may persist, at least to a subtle degree (Petersen and Ghoneim 1980). This impairment may be more common in the first minutes to hours after a dose is taken. Patients must be warned about these more subtle effects, and family and friends may help provide objective evidence if decrements in psychomotor activity or new-learning ability appear. More frequent dosing at decreased dosages may decrease these side effects.

Patients with panic disorder should be started on 0.5 mg PO BID to TID of alprazolam, with increases of 0.5 mg every 2 or 3 days until the panic attacks have stopped. In psychopharmacology clinics, patients generally require 3 mg to 10 mg of alprazolam for effective treatment; however, in primary care, most patients respond at between 1.0 and 3.0 mg of alprazolam. This is probably because they are less severely ill than are patients who are referred to psychiatrists.

Among the other benzodiazepines found to be effective in panic, dosages equivalent to 0.5 mg of alprazolam are 0.25 of clonazepam, 5 mg of diazepam, and 1.0 mg of lorazepam (Roy-Byrne et al. in press). If a short-acting benzodiazepine is used (alprazolam and lorazepam) and the patient breaks through with anxiety attacks despite QID dosing, then switching to a longer acting benzodiazepine such as clonazepam is often effective. Clonazepam, lorazepam, and alprazolam have been associated with breakthrough depression (depression that becomes apparent as anxiety is decreased) in some patients, so the clinician should monitor these symptoms (Charney et al. 1987; Tesar et al. 1987b; Lydiard et al. 1987).

Monoamine Oxidase Inhibitors

The prototypic MAOI that has been studied in panic disorder is phenelzine. Phenelzine may actually be the most effective medication in the treatment of panic disorder, and it is probably the medication of choice in treatment-resistant panic disorder (Sheehan et al. 1980, 1984; Sheehan 1984).

These medications fell into disfavor in the United States because of the so-called "cheese reaction" they can cause (Tollefson 1983). Patients must closely monitor their diet, because foods that contain high amounts of tyramine can interact with the MAOI and cause a sympathomimetic crisis characterized by headache, diaphoresis, mydriasis, hypertension, neuromuscular excitation, and cardiac dysrhythmia. It is generally accepted that this "crisis" is caused by tyramine that is derived from the digestion of food products and enters the bloodstream in high concentrations, presumably because the liver's monoamine oxidase enzymes are inhibited (Tollefson 1983; Blackwell et al. 1967). Tyramine presumably acts by causing the release of the mobile fraction of norepinephrine into the intersynaptic cleft. In recent years, the monoamine oxidase inhibitors have enjoyed a resurgence of use in the United States, and they are generally accepted (with appropriate dietary constraints and caution with the use of certain specific medications) to be safer than formerly thought (Raskin et al. 1974).

The currently used MAOIs (Table 4) inhibit the monoamine oxidase enzymes in all body tissues. The nonhydrazine MAOI, tranylcypromine, is a

Table 4.   Monoamine oxidase inhibitors

Generic	Trade Name	Initial dosage	Maintenance dosage
Phenelzine sulfate	Nardil	15 mg PO BID	45 mg to 90 mg
Tranylcypromine	Parnate	10 mg PO BID	10 mg to 40 mg
Isocarboxazid	Marplan	10 mg PO BID	10 mg to 50 mg

Side effects: Hypertensive reaction, orthostaic hypotension, insomnia, tachycardia, dry mouth, constipation, blurred vision, hepatocellular damange, delayed ejaculation, impotency, edema.

reversible monoamine oxidase inhibitor (albeit slowly), whereas phenelzine and isocarboxazid are irreversible (Roy-Byrne et al. in press). The monoamine oxidase enzyme's function is oxidative deamination within the outer membrane of neuronal mitochondria. It is one of the two major routes for the inactivation of nonmethylated biogenic amines, such as serotonin, norepinephrine, and dopamine (Tollefson 1983). By inhibiting inactivation of these biogenic amines, MAOIs are thought to increase the concentration of vasoactive amines available for synaptic release. However, recent evidence suggests this enzyme inhibition occurs rapidly at subtherapeutic dosages, whereas clinically the MAOIs often take 2 to 4 weeks for their therapeutic action (Roy-Byrne et al. in press). Thus, the mechanism of action is unclear.

MAOIs are well absorbed after an oral dose and undergo acetylation by the liver (Tollefson 1983). The MAOIs do not produce the stimulatory effects that tricyclic antidepressants do in some patients with panic disorder (Lydiard 1988). They also have fewer sedative and anticholinergic effects. In an NIMH study, 1,110 patients on maintenance phenelzine demonstrated no adverse hypertensive reactions (with proper dietary discretion); one case of elevated liver function tests and a small number of anticholinergic side effects were reported (Raskin et al. 1974). This suggests that the prevalence of MAOI side effects has been overestimated.

Blackwell (1967) also documented that even patients ingesting high-risk food products rarely experience hypertensive effects. Insomnia is a common side effect, and encouraging patients to take the drug earlier in the day is often helpful. Other research suggests that low dosage amitriptyline 25 mg PO QHS can decrease the side effect of insomnia and may actually act to prevent the hypertensive reaction induced by tyramine (Pare et al. 1982). Patients with insomnia who will be prescribed amitriptyline need to be tapered off the

Exhibit 11. Dietary restrictions for patients taking monoamine oxidase inhibitors

Foods that must be avoided
>   Beer and wine, particularly Chianti
>   Cheese, except cottage and cream cheese
>   Smoked or pickled fish, especially herring
>   Beef or chicken liver
>   Summer (dry) sausage
>   Fava or broad bean pods (Italian green beans)
>   Yeast vitamin supplements (brewer's yeast)

Foods that are unlikely to cause problems unless large quantities are consumed
>   Other alcoholic beverages
>   Ripe avocado
>   Ripe fresh banana
>   Sour cream
>   Soy sauce
>   Yogurt

Insufficient evidence of adverse interaction
>   Chocolate
>   Figs
>   Meat tenderizers
>   Raisins
>   Yeast breads
>   Coffee, tea, and other caffeine-containing beverages

Source: McCabe, B., and Tsuang, M.T. *Journal of Clinical Psychiatry* 43(5):178-181, 1982. Copyright 1982 Physicians Post-Graduate Press, Inc. Reprinted with permission.

MAOIs and kept off for 7 to 10 days; then they can have small dosages of amitriptyline and the MAOI started at the same time (see below).

Another side effect of MAOIs is orthostatic hypotension, which often begins 3 to 4 weeks after starting the medication (Kopin et al. 1965). Potential mechanisms to decrease hypotension include lowering the dosage, salt tablets, abdominal binders, and the use of fluorodeoxy-corticosterone. Other less common side effects are listed in Table 4.

The hypertensive reaction is the major potential toxicity of the MAOIs. The patient needs to remain on a tyramine-free diet (Exhibit 11) to minimize the risk of this reaction (McCabe and Tsuang 1982). This diet should be continued for 2 weeks after treatment ends, owing to the irreversible inhibition

---

Successful Treatment of Panic Disorder With an MAOI

Mr. M was a 27-year-old businessman who presented with a 6-month history of acute attacks of dyspnea, sweating, tachycardia, tremulousness, and dizziness. He had to make frequent oral presentations at work to groups of colleagues, and the attacks were making these more and more difficult. In addition, he had been avoiding social situations such as parties because the attacks had embarrassed him during several previous social interactions. He was one of seven children, with at least two other siblings suffering from panic disorder. His mother had recurrent severe depressions.

Mr. M was diagnosed as having panic disorder and started on imipramine 25 mg, which was increased to 100 mg over 2 to 3 weeks. He had increased jitteriness and a sense of being "speeded up" on the imipramine, which did not improve over a 1-month period. The imipramine was stopped, and after 10 days, phenelzine was started at 15 mg. The dosage was increased to 60 mg over 2 to 3 weeks with a rapid amelioration of all panic attacks. His anticipatory anxiety with business speeches and presentations and parties gradually decreased over 2 months as he reexperienced these situations and found that he no longer developed anxiety attacks. He has been seen in weekly psychotherapy that has addressed chronic self-esteem problems and his tendency to pressure himself to always be "perfect" to compensate for his low self-concept. His phenelzine was tapered to a maintenance dose of 15 mg during this time.

---

of the MAOIs (Goldberg 1964). The patient must also avoid medications that can precipitate hypertensive crises when used in conjunction with MAOIs. These include sympathomimetic agents of any kind, such as over-the-counter stimulants, amphetamines, many cold tablets containing ephedrine-like compounds, meperidine, cocaine, L-dopa, methyldopa, and asthma inhalants (Pare 1977). Also, it is not safe to switch from one MAOI to another; the first MAOI must be stopped for 10 to 14 days before starting another, or an adrenergic crisis can ensue. Tricyclic antidepressants should not be added to MAOIs that have been already prescribed—they can cause fever, delirium, and seizures (Roy-Byrne et al. in press).

Hypertensive reactions are characterized by severe, crushing, throbbing headache, accompanied by sweating and flushing, nausea and vomiting or neck stiffness and photophobia. Blood pressure increases associated with headache have been about 55 mm systolic and 30 mm diastolic. One useful strategy is to prescribe one to two 10-mg tablets of nifedipine for patients taking MAOIs to carry around at all times for use if a sudden "throbbing" headache associated with these other symptoms occurs (Clary and Schweitzer

1987). Dosages of 5 mg IV of the alpha-adrenergic blocker phentolamine will also reduce the blood pressure.

For the patient with panic disorder, a dosage of 15 mg PO each morning of phenelzine for the first 2 days should be followed by 15 mg PO BID for 1 week. An increase of 15 mg per day should continue each week thereafter until all panic attacks have ceased. The highest daily dosage that should be used is 90 to 105 mg, but most patients improve at 45 to 90 mg.

Length of Treatment and Relapse

Once an effective dosage of a tricyclic antidepressant, MAOI, or benzodiazepine is found and the patient's panic attacks have entirely ceased, the patient should be kept on that medication for 6 to 12 months. The dosage of medication should then be tapered. Tricyclic antidepressants should be tapered by 25 to 50 mg every 1 to 2 weeks. Monoamine oxidase inhibitors should be tapered by 10 to 15 mg (one tablet) per week.

Benzodiazepines appear to be more difficult to taper in patients with panic disorder. A recent placebo-controlled study of alprazolam tapering in patients with panic disorder demonstrated that 27 percent of the alprazolam group reported a rebound of panic attacks and 13 percent had rebound anxiety (Pecknold et al. 1988). No serious or life-threatening withdrawal symptoms were reported, but a distinct, transient mild to moderate withdrawal syndrome occurred in 35 percent of the alprazolam-treated group and in none of the placebo-treated group. The recommendation from this study was to treat panic disorder for at least 6 months and to taper benzodiazepines quite slowly over at least 8 weeks. If the patients receiving benzodiazepines experience recurrence of symptoms, stopping the taper is advised. If the symptoms subside over the next several days, the likely cause was rebound anxiety or withdrawal. The patient can then be gradually withdrawn at a slower rate (Lydiard 1988).

Several additional strategies appear to be helpful in patients with panic disorder when tapering a benzodiazepine has been difficult. Preliminary evidence suggests that the addition of carbamazepine at 400-800 mg daily will decrease benzodiazepine withdrawal symptoms, even if the benzodiazepine is tapered rapidly over 4 to 7 days (Roy-Byrne et al. in press). Alternatively, the addition of a tricyclic antidepressant to therapeutic levels (100 mg to 300 mg) will often decrease the likelihood of rebound panic attacks with tapering of benzodiazepines.

Should the patient relapse during withdrawal or soon after withdrawal of one of the three classes of antipanic medications (and the symptoms do not subside in several days), then another 6- to 12-month course of medication is prescribed before a second attempt to taper medication is instituted.

Many patients find that a smaller dosage of medication is needed for maintenance than for acute treatment. With relapse, the dosage of medication should be increased to just above the level at which relapse occurred, which is often below the highest dosage needed in the past. A small subgroup of patients will need chronic lifelong treatment or will relapse frequently. For these patients, lifelong use of a medication (tricyclic antidepressant, MAOI, or benzodiazepine) is preferable to the frequent relapses or chronic symptoms of panic disorder and their adverse effects on the patient's personal, family, and vocational lives.

Panic disorder, like peptic ulcer disease, is a relapsing, remitting disorder that is often precipitated by stressful life events. Studies have reported that anywhere from 30 to 90 percent of patients relapse within 1 year (Roy-Byrne and Katon 1987). The combination of psychotherapy and medication may decrease this propensity toward relapse because psychotherapy frequently improves self-esteem and successful coping with stress and generally improves the patient's sense of self-efficacy (Bandura 1977).

Psychotherapy

Patients with panic disorder vary considerably in the life stresses that precipitate their disorders; the strength of their social support network; their use of healthy coping mechanisms, such as exercise, recreational hobbies (hiking, swimming, fishing), and relaxation techniques that can decrease the effects of stress; and their baseline self-esteem and coping mechanisms. Brown and colleagues' series of prospective studies have convincingly demonstrated that although patients may have genetic susceptibility to a disorder such as depression or panic disorder, life stresses invariably precipitate the acute episode (Finlay-Jones and Brown 1981). Moreover, patients with chronic poor self-esteem or chronic ongoing problems (such as an unhappy marriage) are at increased risk of developing an episode of panic disorder or major depression should a stressful life event or series of events occur (Brown et al. 1987). Panic disorder may also occur at key developmental transition phases such as leaving home for the first time, after the birth of a first child, or a promotion at work.

Along with social factors, it is useful to determine the patient's psychologic vulnerability to stressful life events. Panic disorder occurs in a wide variety of patients, from those who have many psychological strengths to those with severe personality disorders. Histories of patients' experiences in their family of origin (looking for key factors such as early loss of parents, rejecting parents who provided little nurturance, childhood physical or sexual abuse, parental substance abuse and other mental illness, a family history of panic disorder and/or agoraphobia) and the patients' experience with adult intimate relationships often are quite helpful.

Understanding the social context in which panic disorder developed as well as the psychologic strengths and vulnerabilities of the patient helps to evaluate whether any ongoing problems could be addressed by psychotherapy.

If a marital crisis and potential separation provoked the panic attacks, marital therapy should be initiated. A long-term problem with poor self-esteem, a tendency to have problems with passivity, avoidance, and lack of assertiveness, or recurrent relationships that have led to feelings of rejection would indicate psychodynamic therapy. As with all clinical illness, it is useful for the primary care physician to assess patients with panic disorder utilizing the biopsychosocial model (Figure 9).

Such a model dispenses with the dualism and reductionism of traditional biomedical teaching and replaces the simple cause-and-effect explanations of linear causality with reciprocal causal models (Engel 1977, 1980). The biopsychosocial model expands clinicians' treatment options as well as their understanding and therapeutic alliance with their patients. Somatic symptoms often express patients' distress in many dimensions of their lives, and the job of the clinician is to determine whether the etiology of that distress is in the biologic, social, or psychologic sphere or a combination of the three.

Biosphere
↓ ↑
Society-Nation
↓ ↑
Culture-Subculture
↓ ↑
Community
↓ ↑
Family
↓ ↑
Two-Person
↓ ↑
Person
(experience and behavior)
↓ ↑
Nervous System
↓ ↑
Organs/Organ Systems
↓ ↑
Tissues
↓ ↑
Cells
↓ ↑
Organelles
↓ ↑
Molecules
↓ ↑
Atoms
↓ ↑
Subatomic Particles

Figure 9. The biopsychosocial model. Source: Adapted from Engel, G. L. The clinical application of the biopsychosocial model. *American Journal of Psychiatry* 137:537, 1980. Copyright 1980 by the American Psychiatric Association. Reproduced with permission.

In this model, the patient's symptoms could result from perturbations in their family and marriage and lead to changes at the subcellular level. Alternatively, changes in a tissue or organ (such as ischemia of myocardial tissue) could cause marital or family problems.

Case 1 demonstrates how major perturbations in one's society and nation can dramatically effect one's culture, community, and family, causing overwhelming stress to the individual. Mr. W had both posttraumatic stress disorder and panic disorder. The medication ameliorated his panic attacks, and supportive therapy aimed at ventilation and abreaction of his suffering in the Cambodian revolution helped decrease his psychologic pain as well as cementing the therapeutic alliance.

Panic Disorder and the Biopsychosocial Model 1

Mr. W was a 28-year-old Cambodian refugee who had several emergency room and primary care visits over a 2-month period due to chest pain. He also had a 3-day admission in the coronary care unit where EKG, echocardiogram, and exercise treadmill test were negative. Because of his anxiety, he was referred for psychiatric consultation. He described his chest pain as associated with tachycardia, dyspnea, paresthesia, sweatiness, dizziness, and a fear of heart attack. Mr. W had migrated to Seattle after spending 3 years in a resettlement refugee camp in Thailand. He had been brought up in a middle-class family in Phnom Penh prior to the Communist takeover. After the takeover, he and his four siblings and parents were forcibly marched out of their home in the capital of Cambodia to a rural area and had to work as farmers. There was little food, and his father and one sister died from starvation. Mr. W and his brother escaped by walking more than 200 miles to Thailand, where they spent 3 years in poverty before emigrating to America. Mr. W had tried to contact his mother and two surviving sisters by mail, but had not been able to reach them in 3 years. He had frequent nightmares of their starvation experience and had been bothered by the autonomic episodes described above for over a year.

Mr. W was diagnosed as meeting DSM-III criteria for panic disorder and posttraumatic stress disorder. He was started on imipramine, and his panic episodes rapidly were ameliorated on 100 mg a day. He was also treated with supportive psychotherapy once a week during which he described in depth much of his and his family's suffering over the 3-year period. Eventually, he wrote a 50-page account of this period of his life, and the ventilation and abreaction (reliving the grief and terror of these years) seemed to be quite therapeutic. Mr. W was able to taper and discontinue imipramine after 6 months of treatment, and he has remained asymptomatic for 3 years.

Case 2 demonstrates how a current life stress may bring up overwhelming, painful childhood memories associated with the onset of panic attacks.

In this case, problems with her relationship with her husband had brought up repressed traumatic memories from her family experience and had resulted in overwhelming stress that led to dysregulation of her autonomic nervous system.

To date, no studies have examined the specific efficacy of psychodynamic, marital, or family therapy in patients with panic disorder, either alone or in combination with psychopharmacology (Roy-Byrne and Katon 1987). However, these therapies often decrease social and psychologic distress and improve self-esteem. They also provide models for the use of more appropriate problem-focused coping mechanisms instead of maladaptive mechanisms such as avoidance, wishful thinking, and passivity, which are commonly used by patients with panic disorder. As such, these therapies may decrease the tendency to relapse, as well as decrease the morbidity should panic attacks recur. In major depression, new evidence has suggested that the combination of a psychotherapeutic and psychopharmacologic approach is usually superior to

---

Panic Disorder and the Biopsychosocial Model 2

Mrs. M was a 40-year-old white female who presented to her primary care physician with a 1-month history of insomnia, nightmares, and acute attacks of rapid heartbeat, dizziness, paresthesia, hot flashes, and depersonalization. She wondered if she were "going through the change." Asked about life stresses, Mrs. M reported the onset of her disorder after her husband (she had been married for 15 years and had two children) returned home from work 2 hours late. He had gone out drinking (which was not typical) with his friends after work and had lost track of time. She and her husband got into a verbal argument and he lost his temper and, for the first time in the marriage, slapped her. Mrs. M stated she had gradually forgiven him but, subsequently, whenever her husband attempted to hug or touch her, it would make her skin "crawl" and she would yell at him. Because of her vivid description, she was asked about any past history of physical or sexual abuse. Mrs. M tearfully recounted that she had been both physically and sexually abused as a child by an alcoholic father, and that she had been having nightmares and flashbacks of this trauma since her husband had struck her. Mrs. M was diagnosed as having panic disorder secondary to both marital distress and psychologic vulnerability due to problems in her family of origin. Imipramine, 150 mg a day, stabilized her panic disorder, and Mrs. M was referred for psychodynamic therapy. Over a year's time, she was able to deal with her childhood trauma, which helped stabilize and strengthen her relationship with her husband.

reliance on any single modality (Dimascio et al. 1979), and the same approach is recommended in panic disorder.

Behavioral Therapy

Another specific type of therapy for panic disorder and its sequelae of multiple phobias deserves mention. Pharmacotherapy, by reducing or ameliorating spontaneous anxiety attacks, can quickly relieve suffering and facilitate movement toward reentering phobic situations. A behavioral technique termed *in vivo exposure* does not directly affect the occurrence of panic, but instead, it gradually reduces the anticipatory anxiety felt toward stimuli and situations that have been associated with panic attacks (Marks 1987; Ghosh et al. 1984; Rapee and Barlow 1988; Roberts 1984). As the anticipatory anxiety diminishes and the individual develops a sense of confidence and mastery, the episodes of panic may diminish.

In vivo exposure involves a simple principle—persuading patients to reenter those frightening situations that they have long avoided, and to stay in them long enough (often an hour or more) for the fear to diminish (Marks and Horder 1988). The exposure does not need to occur with a friend, family member, or with the physician.

The primary care physician can carry out this treatment in patients with multiple phobias and/or agoraphobia and panic disorder. The physician must first develop a list with the patient of the specific fears and places that are avoided. He then explains that avoiding situations perpetuates phobias. The rapid avoidance or escape from a feared situation prevents patients from learning that if they just stayed in the situation, the anxiety would subside anyway (Marks and Horder in press). In fact, avoidance and escape make anxiety worse the next time the patient must face a similar situation. The old proverb and folk wisdom about "When you fall off a horse, you should get right back on" is familiar to most people and often helpful. Exposure works better if the patient is able to stay in the situation long enough for the anxiety to lessen.

The primary care physician and the patient should rank the list of fears from the most difficult to the least difficult and then, starting with the least difficult situations, negotiate and agree each week about which specific fears or situations to face. Thus, an agoraphobic might walk one block away from home and stay there for 1 hour the first week; this would be followed by a longer walk to a local shop, and then to more distant locales; next might be riding public transportation, such as buses, and exposure to crowds; finally, the patient would schedule a job interview. Patients are encouraged to keep diaries of their exposure "homework" to bring each week to the physician. It is important to reinforce the patient for successful exposure and to encourage the patient to try again when avoidance has occurred.

Panic Disorder Treated With In Vivo Exposure

Mr. L was a first-year medical student who presented to his primary care physician with episodes of shortness of breath, tachycardia, anxiety, and epigastric pain. Further history revealed these episodes had started while watching a movie of open heart surgery and had quickly generalized to watching movies in theaters and going to large parties. Also, several episodes had occurred during class when patients with particular illnesses were presented. Mr. L's physician explained that avoidance of these situations would lead to more and more anxiety in the future and explained the technique of in vivo exposure. Mr. L felt if he could just have more exposure to patients in a controlled situation in which his instructor knew of his anxiety, he could become desensitized. The physician arranged a once-a-week 2-hour experience with an emergency room physician in which the student would follow this physician's rounds and watch him in his patient care. After 3 weeks, the student reported that he had seen 14 or 15 patients with the emergency room physician and a range of cases from a patient with a severe skull injury to patients with influenza. His anxiety had decreased each week, his confidence had improved, and he no longer reacted with anxiety to classroom movies of medical procedures or patient presentations. Also, in vivo exposure to movies and parties the following few weeks worked quite well to decrease these fears.

Studies have described excellent results for in vivo exposure in both psychiatric and primary care patients as far as decreasing phobic behavior (Marks 1987). It is not entirely clear whether these patients' panic attacks go away with effective exposure treatment; however, in some patients, this treatment is probably effective for both spontaneous panic attacks and for agoraphobia (Marks and Horder in press; Roberts 1984). Its ease and low cost make this procedure a useful alternative for patients who refuse to take medications or as an adjunct to pharmacotherapy. Several studies have suggested the possibility that the behavioral treatment and tricyclic antidepressant treatment may both be effective because they act on similar receptors (Marks and Tobena 1986). Exposure to repeated stress in rodents leads to a gradual decrease in physiologic and behavioral responses to that stress and correlates with widespread down-regulation or decrease in central beta-adrenergic postsynaptic receptor sensitivity (Stone 1983). Tricyclic antidepressants also cause down-regulation of beta-adrenergic postsynaptic receptors and decrease panic attacks and phobic behavior (Charney et al. 1981*b*).

Several groups are experimenting with new methods of behavioral therapy to add to in vivo exposure. Many authors have reported that patients with panic disorder seem to have a "fear of fear" (Clark 1986*a, b;* Rapee and Barlow

1988; Hibbert 1984). That is, their panic attacks are so frightening that any somatic symptom that reminds them of a panic attack (such as rapid heartbeat or sweating) may lead to the sudden increase of anxiety and a subsequent panic attack.

One researcher demonstrated that in a patient with panic disorder attached to a biofeedback heart monitor, the bogus report that his heart rate was increasing led to panic attacks (Margraf et al. 1987). Weekes (1976) has described the phenomenon of sensitization in patients with panic attacks whereby the autonomic and somatic sensory nerves react to internal organ signals (missed or ectopic heartbeat, heartburn, giddy stomach, epigastric distress) with heightened nervous sensations and often excessively strong and precipitant emotional responses (anxiety attacks).

Several groups have reported good results with therapy in which the patient exercises or hyperventilates to provoke internal physiologic cues associated with panic attacks (Rapee and Barlow 1988; Salkovskis et al. 1986). The patient is gradually exposed and habituated to these cues in the same way agoraphobic patients are gradually exposed and desensitized to external cues associated with panic. Patients are also taught to slow down their breathing as a mechanism to decrease symptoms of hyperventilation. Barlow and Craske (1989) have recently developed a self-programmed manual called *Mastery of Your Anxiety and Panic* that helps patients understand their anxiety and provides exercises (such as the hyperventilation exercise) that provoke panic symptoms and teach the patient to develop mastery over these physiologic sensations.

Panic Disorder Treated With Hyperventilation Exposure and Breathing Training

Mrs. B was a 35-year-old married black female who presented to the emergency room four times in 2 weeks with shortness of breath, chest pain, tachycardia, sweatiness, and fear that she was having a heart attack. These attacks started after her best friend, a 40-year-old female, died suddenly from a myocardial infarction. Mrs. B was told she had panic disorder and was hyperventilating. She doubted this diagnosis, stating she breathed fast because she felt she couldn't catch her breath. She was instructed to breathe at 40 to 60 breaths per minute in the office. This precipitated her exact symptoms and convinced her she was hyperventilating. Mrs. B was then taught to breath "by the watch" at a rate of one breath every 5 seconds to stop a panic attack or hyperventilation episode. Several trials of rapid breathing followed by breathing once every 5 seconds were tried in the office, teaching her to ameliorate her own attacks. The patient had a rapid recovery and no medication was required.

A useful behavioral strategy in primary care in both diagnosis and treatment may be to ask the patient to breathe in and out rapidly at 40 to 60 breaths per minute to see if hyperventilation simulates the presenting symptoms. Patients are then taught to slow down their breathing to a normal 15 to 20 respirations per minute by timed breathing (i.e., one breath every 5 seconds) rather than their internal breathing cues. Repeated trials of having the patient hyperventilate to provoke symptoms, then slowing down the breathing to ameliorate symptoms seems to allow some patients to gain control of panic attacks. Uncontrolled studies have found this behavioral method quite successful (Rapee and Barlow 1988; Lum 1971).

These simple behavioral techniques are helpful to convince the patient of the diagnosis. In some patients with less severe disorders, they seem to be curative. Controlled trials of behavioral treatments that desensitize patients to their own somatic symptoms have not been reported, but many case reports in the literature suggest that these techniques are quite helpful (Roy-Byrne and Katon 1987).

Indications for Psychiatric Consultation or Referral

Although most patients with panic disorder can be successfully treated in primary care, some cases would benefit from psychiatric consultation or referral:

- In patients with panic disorder who present with one or more somatic complaints, such as chest pain or irritable bowel syndrome, and tend to deny or minimize stressful life events and anxiety, diagnosis can be difficult. A psychiatric consultation may help confirm the diagnosis of panic disorder as well as elucidate family relationships, alcohol and drug history, affective illness, or somatoform disorders that are part of the patient's problem (Katon 1986).
- Many patients with panic disorder can have their panic attacks treated psychopharmacologically within the primary care system. A small subgroup of patients have treatment-resistant panic attacks or are hypersensitive to the side effects of psychopharmacologic agents. They may benefit from psychiatric consultation and/or referral.
- Patients with panic disorder frequently also suffer from major depression as well as demoralization about the overwhelming nature of their anxiety attacks. It is not unusual to see patients with either panic disorder alone or panic disorder and major depression who have serious suicidal ideation and a suicide plan. Coryell and colleagues' (1982) 20-year followup study of patients with panic disorder suggested that these patients are more apt to die from suicide than are controls. Psychiatric consultation and/or referral should usually be sought in this subgroup of patients.
- Some patients with panic disorder have serious medical illness such as heart disease, diabetes, or chronic obstructive lung disease that may complicate psychopharmacologic treatment of panic attacks.

Also, the medications the patient needs to take for the chronic medical condition may interact with the therapeutic medications used for panic disorder. A psychiatric consultation or referral is often helpful to determine the safest possible psychopharmacologic treatment to prescribe.

- Patients with panic disorder who have a strong family history of alcoholism, affective disorders, or suicide or a personal history of alcoholism, substance abuse/dependence, erratic behavior or personality disorder, or psychotic illness would benefit from psychiatric consultation and/or referral.
- In panic disorder complicated by agoraphobia, psychopharmacologic amelioration of panic disorder and supportive therapy aimed at pushing the patient to confront formerly phobic situations usually gradually decrease avoidance behavior and phobic patterns. In recalcitrant patients who are too fearful to reenter phobic situations despite effective pharmacologic blockade of acute panic attacks, referral to a behaviorally oriented psychotherapist is often quite helpful.

Suggested Readings

Articles for Patients and Physicians

Katon, W. Panic disorder: Epidemiology, diagnosis and treatment in primary care. *Journal of Clinical Psychiatry* 47(10 suppl):21-27, 1987.

Katon, W.; Sheehan, D.; and Uhde, T.W. Panic disorder: A treatable problem. *Patient Care.* March 30:148-173, 1988.

National Insititute of Mental Health. *Panic and Phobias.* Pub. No. (ADM) 87-1472. Rockville, MD: the Institute, 1987.

Books for Patients and Physicians

Barlow, D.H., and Craske, M.G. *Mastery of Your Anxiety and Panic.* New York: Center for Stress and Anxiety Disorders, State University of New York at Albany, 1989.

Marks, I.M. *Living With Fear.* New York: McGraw-Hill, 1978.

Sheehan, D.V. *The Anxiety Disease.* New York: Bantam Books, 1986.

Weeks, C. *Hope and Help for Your Nerves.* New York: Bantam Books, 1978.

Wender, P., and Klein, D. *Mind, Mood and Medicine.* New York: Farrar, Strauss and Giroux, 1981.

Computer Software for Physicians

Katon, W. *Chest Pain in a 30-Year-Old-Man.* CME, Incorporated, P.O. Box 85655, Seattle, WA 98145-1655. Telephone: 203-543-2259.

Bibliography

Abraham, H.D. "BEAM Studies in Panic Disorder: An Exploration." Paper presented at the 141st Annual Meeting of the American Psychiatric Association, Montreal, 1988.

Ackerman, J.H., and Sachar, E.J. The lactate theory of anxiety: A review and reevaluation. *Psychosomatic Medicine* 36:69-81, 1974.

Adams, J.R.; Wahby, V.S.; Giller, E.L.; and Mason, J.W. "Free Thyroid Levels in Patients with Panic Disorder." Paper presented at the 42nd Annual Meeting of the American Psychosomatic Society, Washington, DC, 1985.

Aghajanian, G.K. Tolerance of locus coeruleus neurons to morphine and suppression of withdrawal response by clonidine. *Nature* 276:186-188, 1978.

American Psychiatric Association. *Diagnostic and Statistical Manual of Mental Disorders. Third Edition, Revised.* Washington, DC: APA, 1987.

Amsterdam, J.; Brunswick, D.; and Mendels, J. The clinical application of tricyclic antidepressant pharmacokinetics and plasma levels. *American Journal of Psychiatry* 137:653-659, 1980.

Andrade, R., and Aghajanian, G.K. Intrinsic regulation of locus coeruleus neurons: Electrophysiologic evidence of a predominant role for auto-inhibition. *Brain Research* 310:401-106, 1984.

Andreasen, N.C.; Endicott, J.; Spitzer, R.L.; and Winokur, G. The family history method using diagnostic criteria. *Archives of General Psychiatry* 34:1229-1235, 1977.

Appleby, I.L.; Klein, D.F.; Sachar, E.J.; and Levitt, M. Biochemical indices of lactate-induced panic: A preliminary report. In: Klein, D.F., and Rabkin, J., eds. *Anxiety: New Research and Changing Concepts.* New York: Raven Press, 1981.

Aronson, T.A., and Craig, T.J. Cocaine precipitation of panic disorder. *American Journal of Psychiatry* 143:643-645, 1986.

Arrindel, W.A.; Emmelkamp, P.M.G.; Monsma, A.; and Brilman, E. The role of perceived parental rearing practices in the aetiology of phobic disorders: A controlled study. *British Journal of Psychiatry* 143:183-187, 1983.

Ballenger, J.C.; Peterson, G.A.; and Laraia, C. A study of plasma catecholamines in agoraphobia and the relationship of serum tricyclic levels to treatment response. In: Ballenger, J.C., ed. Biology of Agoraphobia. Washington, DC: American Psychiatric Press, 1984. p. 42.

Ballenger, J.C.; Gibson, R.; Peterson, G.A.; and Laraia, M.T. "'Functional' MVP in Agoraphobia/Panic Disorder." Paper presented at the 139th Annual Meeting of the American Psychiatric Association, Washington, DC, 1986.

Ballenger, J.C.; Burrows, G.D.; Dupont, R.L., Jr.; Lesser, I.M.; Noyes, R., Jr.; Pecknold, J.C.; Rifkin, A.; and Swinson, R.P. Alprazolam in panic disorder and agoraphobia: Results from a multicenter trial. I. Efficacy in short-term treatment. Archives of General Psychiatry 45:413-422, 1988.

Balon R.; Ortiz, A.; Pohl, R.; and Yeragani, V.K. Heart rate and blood pressure during placebo-associated panic attacks. Psychosomatic Medicine 50:434-438, 1988.

Bandura, A. Self-efficacy: Towards a unifying theory of behavioral change. Psychological Review 84:191-215, 1977.

Barlow, D.H., and Craske, M. Mastery of Your Anxiety and Panic. Center for Stress and Anxiety Disorders, State University of New York at Albany, 1989.

Barlow, D.H.; Blanchard, E.B.; Vermilyea, J.A.; Vermilyea, B.B.; and Dinardo, P.A. Generalized anxiety and generalized anxiety disorder: Description and reconceptualization. American Journal of Psychiatry 143:40-44, 1986.

Barlow, J.B.; Bosman, C.K.; Pocock, W.A.; and Marchand, P. Late systolic murmers and non-ejection (mid-late) systolic clicks: An analyses of 90 patients. British Heart Journal 30:203-218, 1968.

Bass, C., and Wade C. Chest pain with normal coronary arteries: A comparative study of psychiatric and social morbidity. Psychosomatic Medicine 14:51-61, 1984.

Beaconsfield, P.; Ginsburg, J.; and Rainsbury, R. Marijuana smoking: Cardiovascular effects in man and possible mechanisms. New England Journal of Medicine 287:209-212, 1972.

Beard, G.M. Practical Treatise on Nervous Exhaustion (Neurasthenia). New York: William Wood, 1880.

Beck, A.T. Cognitive Therapy and the Emotional Disorders. New York: International Universities Press, 1976.

Beitman, B.D.; Basha, I.; Flaker, G.; DeRosear, L.; Mukerji, V.; Trombka, L.; and Katon, W. Atypical or nonanginal chest pain: Panic disorder or coronary artery disease. Archives of Internal Medicine 147:1548-1552, 1987.

Berg, I.; Butler, A.; and Pritchard, J. Psychiatric illness in the mothers of school-phobic and adolescents. British Journal of Psychiatry 125:466-467, 1974.

Berger, A.J.; Mitchell, R.A.; and Severinghaus, J.W. Regulation of respiration. *New England Journal of Medicine* 297:138-143, 1977.

Berkowitz, B.A.; Tarver, J.H.; and Spector, S. Release of norepinephrine in the central nervous system by theophylline and caffeine. *European Journal of Pharmacology* 10:64-71, 1970.

Bigger, J.T., Jr.; Giardina, E.G.V.; Perel, J.M.; Kantor, S.J.; and Glasman, A.H. Cardiac antiarrhythmic effect of imipramine hydrochloride. *New England Journal of Medicine* 296:206-208, 1977.

Bigger, J.T., Jr.; Kantor, S.J.; Glassman, A.H.; and Perel, J.M. Cardiovascular effects of tricyclic antidepressant drugs. In: Lipton, M.A.; DiMascio, A.; and Killam, K.F., eds. *Psychopharmacology: A Generation of Progress.* New York: Raven Press, 1978. pp. 1033-1046.

Bird, S.J., and Kuhar, M.J. Iontophoretic application of opiates to the locus coeruleus. *Brain Research* 122:523-533, 1977.

Black, D.W.; Warrack, G.; and Winokur, G. The Iowa record-linkage study. III. Excess mortality among patients with "functional disorders." *Archives of General Psychiatry* 42:82-88, 1985.

Blackwell, B.; Marley, E.; Price, J.; and Taylor, D. Hypertensive interactions between monoamine oxidase inhibitors and foodstuffs. *British Journal of Psychiatry* 113:349-365, 1967.

Bleich, A.; Siegel, B.; Garb, R.; and Lehrer, B. Post-traumatic stress disorder following combat exposure: Clinical features and psychopharmacologic treatment. *British Journal of Psychiatry* 149:365-369, 1986.

Boulenger, J.P.; Uhde, T.W.; Wolffe, E.A.; and Post, R.M. Increased sensitivity to caffeine in patients with panic disorders. *Archives of General Psychiatry* 41:1067-1071, 1984.

Bowen, R.C.; Cipywny, K.D.; D'Aray, C.; and Keegan, D. Alcoholism, anxiety disorders and agoraphobia. *Alcoholism: Clinical and Experimental Research* 8:48-50, 1984.

Bowlby, J. *Attachment and Loss.* Vol. 2. *Separation: Anxiety and Anger.* London: Hogarth Press, 1973.

Boyd, J.H.; Burke, J.D.; Gruenberg, E.; Holzer, C.E.; Rae, D.S.; George, L.K.; Karno, M.; Stolzman, R.; McEvoy, L.; and Nestadt, G. Exclusion criteria of DSM-III. *Archives of General Psychiatry* 41:983-989, 1984.

Breir, A.; Charney, D.S.; and Heninger, G.B. Major depression in patients with agoraphobia and panic disorder. *Archives of General Psychiatry* 41:1129-1135, 1984.

Breslau, N., and Davis, G.C. DSM-III generalized anxiety disorder: An empirical investigation of more stringent criteria. *Psychiatry Research* 14:231-238, 1985.

Bridges, K.W., and Goldberg, D.P. Somatic presentation of DSM-III psychiatric disorders in primary care. *Journal of Psychosomatic Research* 29:563-569, 1985.

Brown, G.T.; Bifulco, A.; Harris, T.; and Bridge, L. Life stress, chronic subclinical symptoms and vulnerability to clinical depression. *Journal of Affective Disorders* 11:1-19, 1986.

Brown, G.W.; Bifulco, A.; and Harris, T.O. Life events, vulnerability and onset of depression: Some refinements. *British Journal of Psychiatry* 150:30-42, 1987.

Burton, T. *The Anatomy of Melancholy*. New York: Empire State, 1924. p. 172.

Butcher, R.W., and Sutherland, E.W. Adenosine 3',5'-phosphate in biologic materials. *Journal of Biological Chemistry* 237:1244-1250, 1962.

Cameron, O.; Lee, M.A.; Curtis, G.C.; and McCann, D.S. Endocrine and physiologic changes during "spontaneous" panic attacks. *Psychoneuroendocrinology* 12:321-331, 1987.

Cannon, W. *Bodily Changes in Pain, Hunger, Fear, and Rage*. New York: Appleton Century Crofts, 1953.

Carlsson, A.; Holmin, T.; Lindqvist, M.; and Siesjo, B.K. Effect of hypercapnia and hypocapnia on tryptophan and tyrosine hydroxylation in rat brain. *Acta Physiologica Scandinavica* 99:503-509, 1977.

Carr, D.B., and Sheehan, D.V. Panic anxiety: A new biological model. *Journal of Clinical Psychiatry* 45:323-330, 1984.

Carr, D.B.; Sheehan, D.V.; Surman, O.S.; Coleman, J.H.; Greenblatt, D.J.; Heninger, R.G.; Levine, P.H.; and Watkins, W.D. Neuroendocrine correlates of lactate-induced anxiety and their response to chronic alprazolam therapy. *American Journal of Psychiatry* 143:483-494, 1986.

Caughey, J.L. Cardiovascular neurosis—A review. *Psychosomatic Medicine* 1:311-324, 1939.

Cedarbaum, J.M., and Aghajanian, G.K. Catecholamine receptors on locus coeruleus neurons: Pharmacologic considerations. *European Journal of Pharmacology* 44:375-385, 1977.

Channick, B.J.; Adlin, V.E.; Marks, A.D.; Denenberg, B.S.; McDonough, M.T.; Chakko, C.S.; and Spann, J.F. Hyperthyroidism and mitral-valve prolapse. *New England Journal of Medicine* 305:497-500, 1981.

Charney, D.S., and Heninger, G.R. Noradrenergic function and the mechanism of action of antianxiety treatment. *Archives of General Psychiatry* 42:458-467, 1985.

Charney, D.S., and Heninger, G.R. Abnormal regulation of noradrenergic function in panic disorders. *Archives of General Psychiatry* 43:1042-1054, 1986.

Charney, D.S.; Menkes, D.B.; and Heninger, G.R. Receptor sensitivity and the mechanism of action of antidepressant treatment. *Archives of General Psychiatry* 38:1160-1180, 1981a.

Charney, D.S.; Heninger, G.R.; Sternberg, D.E.; Hafstad, K.M.; Giddings, S.; and Landis, D.H. Plasma MHPG in depression: Effects of acute and chronic administration of desipramine treatment. *Psychiatry Research* 5:217-229, 1981*b*.

Charney, D.S.; Heninger, G.R.; and Sternberg, D.E. Assessment of alpha-2 adrenergic autoreceptor function in humans: Effects of oral yohimbine. *Life Sciences* 30:2033-2041, 1982.

Charney, D.S.; Heninger, G.R.; and Breier, A. Noradrenergic function in panic anxiety: Effects of yohimbine in healthy subjects and patients with agoraphobia and panic disorder. *Archives of General Psychiatry* 41:751-763, 1984.

Charney, D.S.; Heninger, G.R.; and Jatlow, P.I. Increased anxiogenic effects of caffeine in panic disorders. *Archives of General Psychiatry* 42:233-243, 1985.

Charney, D.S.; Woods, S.W.; and Goodman, W.K. "The Efficacy of Lorazepam in Panic Disorders." Paper presented at the 140th Annual Meeting of the American Psychiatric Association, Chicago, 1987.

Clancy, J., and Noyes, R. Anxiety neurosis: A disease for the medical model. *Psychosomatics* 17:90-93, 1976.

Clark, D.M. A cognitive approach to panic. *Behaviour Research and Therapy* 24:461-470, 1986*a*.

Clark, D.M. Cognitive therapy for anxiety. *Behavioral Psychotherapy* 14:283-294, 1986*b*.

Clary, C., and Schweitzer, E. Treatment of MAOI hypertensive crisis with sublingual nifedipine. *Journal of Clinical Psychiatry* 48:249-250, 1987.

Cloninger, C.R.; Martin, R.L.; Clayton, P.; and Guze, S.B. A blind follow-up and family study of anxiety neurosis. Preliminary analyses of the St. Louis 500. In: Klein, D.F., and Rabkin, J., eds. *Anxiety: New Research and Changing Concepts.* New York: Raven Press, 1981. pp. 137-148.

Cohen, M.E., and White, P.D. Life situations, emotions and neurocirculatory asthenia (anxiety neurosis, neurasthenia, effort syndrome). *Research Publications Association of Nervous and Mental Diseases* 29:832-869, 1950.

Cohen, M.E.; Badal, D.; Kilpatrick, A.; Reed, E.W.; and White, P.D. The high familial prevalence of neurocirculatory asthenia (anxiety neurosis, effort syndrome). *American Journal of Human Genetics* 3:126-158, 1951.

Collyer, J. Psychosomatic illness in a solo family practice. *Psychosomatics* 20:762-767, 1979.

Coryell, W.; Noyes, R.; and Clancy, J. Excess mortality in panic disorder. *Archives of General Psychiatry* 39:701-703, 1982.

Coryell, W.; Noyes, R.; and House, J.D. Mortality among outpatients with panic disorder. *American Journal of Psychiatry* 143:508-510, 1986.

Costa, P.T.; Zonderman, A.B.; Engel, B.T.; Baile, W.F.; Brimlow, D.L.; and Brinker, J. The relation of chest pain symptoms to angiographic findings of coronary artery stenosis and neuroticism. *Psychosomatic Medicine* 47:285-295, 1985.

Cowley, D., and Roy-Byrne, P.P. Panic disorder: Psychosocial aspects. *Psychiatric Annals* 18:464-467, 1988.

Cowley, D.; Hyde, T.; Dager, S.; and Dunner, D.L. Lactate infusions: The role of baseline anxiety. *Psychiatry Research* 21(2):169-179, 1987*a*.

Cowley, D.; Dager, S.; and Dunner, D. Lactate infusions in major depression without panic attacks. *Journal of Psychiatric Research* 21(3):243-248, 1987*b*.

Craske, M.G., and Barlow, D.H. Nocturnal panic. *Journal of Nervous and Mental Disease* 177:160-167, 1989.

Crowe, R.R. The role of genetics in the etiology of panic disorder. In: Grinspoon, L., ed. *Psychiatry Update*, Vol. 3. Washington, DC: American Psychiatric Press, 1984.

Crowe, R.R.; Noyes, R.; Pauls, D.L.; and Slymen, D.J. A family study of panic disorder. *Archives of General Psychiatry* 40:1065-1069, 1983.

Culpin, M. The psychological aspect of the effort syndrome. *Lancet* ii:184-186, 1920.

D'Aulaire, I., and D'Aulaire, E.P. *Book of Greek Myths*. New York: Doubleday, 1962.

DaCosta, J.M. On irritable heart: A clinical study of a functional cardiac disorder and its consequences. *American Journal of the Medical Sciences* 61:17-52, 1871.

Dager, S.R.; Comess, K.A.; Saal, A.K.; and Dunner, D.L. Mitral valve prolapse in a psychiatric setting: Diagnostic assessment, research and clinical implications. *Integrated Psychiatry* 4:211-213, 1986.

Demers, R.Y.; Altamore, R.; Mustin, H.; Kleinman, A.; and Leonardi, D. An exploration of the dimensions of illness behavior. *Journal of Family Practice* 11:1085-1094, 1980.

Densen, P.M.; Shapiro, S.; and Einhorn, M. Concerning high and low utilizers of services in a medical care plan, and the persistence of utilization levels over a three year period. *Milbank Quarterly* 37(3):217-250, 1959.

Devereux, R.B.; Perloff, J.K.; Reichek, N.; and Josephson, M.E. Mitral valve prolapse. *Circulation* 54:3-14, 1976.

Dimascio, A.; Weissman, M.M.; Prusoff, B.A.; Neu, C.; Swilling, M.; and Klerman, G.L. Differential symptom reduction by drugs and psychotherapy in acute depression. *Archives of General Psychiatry* 36:1450-1456, 1979.

Dirks, J.F.; Schraa, J.C.; and Brown, E. Psycho-maintenance in asthma: Hospitalization rates and financial impact. *British Journal of Medical Psychology* 53:349-354, 1980.

Drossman, D.A.; Sandler, R.S.; McKee, D.C.; and Lovitz, A.J. Bowel patterns among subjects not seeking medical care: Use of a questionnaire to identify a population with bowel dysfunction. *Gastroenterology* 83:529-534, 1982.

Drossman, D.A.; McKee, D.C.; Sandler, R.S.; Mitchel, C.M.; Cramer, E.M.; Lowman, B.C.; and Burger, A.L. Psychosocial factors in the irritable bowel syndrome: A multivariate study of patients and nonpatients with irritable bowel syndrome. *Gastroenterology* 95:701-708, 1988.

Drury, A.N. The percentage of carbon dioxide in the alveolar air, and the tolerance to accumulation of carbon dioxide in cases of so-called "irritable heart." *Heart* 165:1918-1920, 1987.

Dunner, D.L.; Ishiki, D.; Avery, D.H.; Wilson, L.J.; and Hyde, T.S. Effect of alprazolam and diazepam in patients with panic disorder. A controlled study. *Journal of Clinical Psychiatry* 47:458-460, 1986.

Elam, M.; Yao, T.; Thoren, P.; and Svensson, T.H. Hypercapnia and hypoxia: Chemoreceptor mediated control of locus coeruleus neurons and splanchnic sympathetic nerves. *Brain Research* 222:373-381, 1981.

Elam, M.; Yau, T.; Svensson, T.H.; and Thoren, P. Regulation of locus coeruleus neurons and splanchnic sympathetic nerves by cardiovascular afferents. *Brain Research* 290:282-287, 1984.

Elam, M.; Svensson, T.H.; and Thoren, P. Locus coeruleus neurons and sympathetic nerves: Activation by visceral afferents. *Brain Research* 375:117-125, 1986.

Elias, M.F.; Robbins, M.A.; Blow, F.C.; Rice, A.P.; and Edgecomb, J.L. Symptom reporting, anxiety and depression in arteriographically classified middle-aged chest pain patients. *Experimental Aging Research* 8:45-51, 1982.

Emmelkamp, P.M.G., and Kuipers, A.C.M. Agoraphobia: A follow-up study four years after treatment. *British Journal of Psychiatry* 134:352-355, 1979.

Enero, M.A., and Saidman, B.Q. Possible feedback inhibition of noradrenaline release by purine compounds. *Naunyn Schmiedebergs Archives of Pharmacology* 297:39-46, 1977.

Engel, G.L. The need for a new medical model: A challenge for biomedicine. *Science* 196:129-135, 1977.

Engel, G.L. The clinical application of the biopsychosocial model. *American Journal of Psychiatry* 137:537, 1980.

Evans, I.M. A conditioning model of a common neurotic pattern: Fear of fear. *Psychotherapy: Theory, Research, and Practice* 9:238-241, 1972.

Faravelli, D. Life events preceding the onset of panic disorder. *Journal of Affective Disorders* 9:103-105, 1985.

Fava, G.A.; Kellner, R.; Zielezny, M.; and Grandi, S. Hypochondriacal fears and beliefs in agoraphobia. *Journal of Affective Disorders* 14:239-244, 1988.

Finlay-Jones, R., and Brown, G.W. Types of stressful life events and the onset of anxiety and depressive disorders. *Psychological Medicine* 11:803-815, 1981.

Fishman, S.M.; Sheehan, D.V.; and Carr, D.B. Thyroid indices in panic disorder. *Journal of Clinical Psychiatry* 46:432-433, 1985.

Folgering, H., and Colla, P. Some anomalies in the control of $PaCO_2$ in patients with hyperventilation syndrome. *Bulletin Europeen De Physiopathologie Respiratoire* 14:503-512, 1978.

Fontaine, R.; Breton, G.; Fontaine, S.; Elie, R.; and Dery, R. "MRI in Panic Disorders: Atrophy and Decreased Signal in T_1." Paper presented at the 141st Annual Meeting of the American Psychiatric Association, Montreal, 1988.

Ford, C.; Bray, G.A.; and Swerdloff, R.S. A psychiatric study of patients referred with a diagnosis of hypoglycemia. *American Journal of Psychiatry* 133:290-294, 1976.

Ford, D. "The Relationship of Psychiatric Illness to Medically Unexplained Chest Pain." Paper presented at Mental Disorders in General Health Care Settings: A Research Conference, Seattle, 1987.

Fraser, F., and Wilson, R.M. The sympathetic nervous system and the "irritable heart of soldiers." *British Medical Journal* ii:27-29, 1918.

Frazer, A., and Conway, P. Pharmacologic mechanism of action of antidepressants. *Psychiatric Clinics of North America* 7:575-586, 1974.

Freedman, R.R.; Janni, P.; Ettedgui, E.; and Puthezhath, W. Ambulatory monitoring of panic disorder. *Archives of General Psychiatry* 42:244-248, 1985.

Freud, S. On the grounds for detaching a particular syndrome from neurasthenia under the description "anxiety neurosis." *The Standard Edition of the Complete Psychological Works of Sigmund Freud*. Vol. 3 (1893-1899). London: Hogarth, 1894. pp. 76-106.

Frohlich, E.D.; Dustan, H.P.; and Page, I.H. Hyperdynamic beta-adrenergic circulatory state. *Archives of Internal Medicine* 117:614-619, 1966.

Fyer, A.J.; Liebowitz, M.R.; Gorman, J.M.; Campeas, R.; Levin, A.; Davies, S.O.; Goetz, D.; and Klein, D.F. Discontinuation of alprazolam treatment in panic patients. *American Journal of Psychiatry* 144:303-308, 1987.

Garcia de Yebenes Prous, J.; Carlsson, A.; and Mena Gomez, M.A. The effect of CO_2 on monoamine metabolism in rat brain. *Naunym Schmiedebergs Archives of Pharmacology* 301:11-15, 1977.

George, D.T.; Zerby, A.; Noble, S.; and Nutt, D.J. Panic attacks and alcohol withdrawal: Can subjects differentiate the symptoms? *Biological Psychiatry* 24:240-243, 1988.

Ghadirian, A.M.; Gauthier, S.; and Bertrand, S. Anxiety attacks in a patient with a right temporal lobe meningioma. *Journal of Clinical Psychiatry* 47:270-271, 1986.

Ghosh, A.; Marks, I.M.; and Carr, A.C. Controlled study of self-exposure treatment for phobics. *Journal of the Royal Society of Medicine* 77:483-487, 1984.

Gilbert, R.M. Caffeine: Overview and anthology. In: Miller, S.A., ed. *Nutrition and Behavior*. Philadelphia: Franklin Institute Press, 1981. pp. 145-166.

Gillette, P.C.; Smith, R.T.; Garson, A.; Mullins, C.E.; Gutgesell, H.P.; Goh, T.H.; Cooley, D.A.; and McNamara, D.G. Chronic supraventricular tachycardia: A curable cause of congestive cardiomyopathy. *Journal of the American Medical Association* 253:391-392, 1985.

Ginsborg, B.L., and Hirst, G.D.S. The effect of adenosine on the release of transmitter from the phrenic nerve of the rat. *Journal of Physiology* 224:629-645, 1972.

Gittelman, R., and Klein, D.F. Childhood separation anxiety and adult agoraphobia. In: Tuma, A.H., and Maser, J., eds. *Anxiety and the Anxiety Disorders*. Hillsdale, New Jersey: Lawrence Erlbaum, 1985.

Glassman, A.H.; Giardana, E.V.; Pekel, J.M.; Bigger, J.T., Jr.; Kantor, S.J.; and Davies, M. Clinical characteristics of imipramine-induced orthostatic hypotension. *Lancet* i:468-472, 1979.

Glassman, A.H.; Johnson, L.L.; Giardina, E.G.; Walsh, B.T.; Roose, S.P.; Cooper, T.B.; and Bigger, J.T., Jr. The use of imipramine in depressed patients with congestive heart failure. *Journal of American Medical Association* 250:1997-2001, 1983.

Gloger, S.; Grunhaus, L.; Birmacher, B.; and Troudart, T. Treatment of spontaneous panic attacks with clomipramine. *American Journal of Psychiatry* 138:1215-1217, 1981.

Gloor, P.; Olivier, A.; Quesney, L.F.; Andermann, F.; and Horowitz, S. The role of the limbic system in experiential phenomena of temporal lobe epilepsy. *Annals of Neurology* 12:129-144, 1982.

Goldberg, D. Detection and assessment of emotional disorders in a primary care setting. *International Journal of Mental Health* 8:30-48, 1979.

Goldberg, L.I. Monoamine oxidase inhibitors: Adverse reactions and possible mechanisms. *Journal of American Medical Association* 190:132-138, 1964.

Gorlin, R. The hyperkinetic heart syndrome. *Journal of the American Medical Association* 182:823-829, 1962.

Gorman, J.M., and Martinez, J.M. Hypoglycemia and panic attacks. *American Journal of Psychiatry* 141:101-102, 1984.

Gorman, J.M.; Fyer, A.F.; Gliklick, J.; King, D.L.; and Klein, D.F. Effect of imipramine on prolapsed mitral valves of patients with panic disorder. *American Journal of Psychiatry* 138:977-978, 1981a.

Gorman, J.M.; Fyer, A.F.; Gliklick, J.; King, D.L.; and Klein, D.F. Effect of sodium lactate on patients with panic disorder and mitral valve prolapse. *American Journal of Psychiatry* 138:247-249, 1981b.

Gorman, J.M.; Levy, G.F; Liebowitz, M.R.; McGrath, P.; Appleby, I.L.; Dillon, D.J.; Davies, S.O.; and Klein, D.F. The effect of acute beta-adrenergic blockade on lactate-induced panic. *Archives of General Psychiatry* 40:1079-1082, 1983.

Gorman, J.M.; Askanazi, J.; Liebowitz, M.R.; Fyer, A.J.; Stein, J.; Kinney, J.M.; and Klein, D.F. Response to hyperventilation in a group of patients with panic disorder. *American Journal of Psychiatry* 141:857-861, 1984.

Gorman, J.M.; Cohen, B.S.; Liebowitz, M.R.; Fyer, A.J.; Ross, D.; Davies, S.O.; and Klein, O.F. Blood gas changes and hypophosphatemia in lactate-induced panic. *Archives of General Psychiatry* 43:1067-1071, 1986*a*.

Gorman, J.M.; Shear, M.K.; Devereux, R.B.; King, D.L.; and Klein, D.F. Prevalence of mitral valve prolapse in panic disorder: Effect of echocardiographic criteria. *Psychosomatic Medicine* 48:167-171, 1986*b*.

Gorman, J.M.; Liebowitz, M.R.; Fyer, A.J.; Fyer, M.R.; and Klein, D.F. Possible respiratory abnormalities in panic disorder. *Psychopharmacology Bulletin* 22:797-801, 1986*c*.

Gorman, J.M.; Fyer, M.R.; Goetz, R., Askanazi, J.; Liebowitz, M.R.; Fyer, A.J.; Kinney, J.; and Klein, D.F. Ventillatory physiology of patients with panic disorder. *Archives of General Psychiatry* 45:31-39, 1988*a*.

Gorman, J.M.; Goetz, R.R.; Fyer, M.; King, D.L.; Fyer, A.J.; Liebowitz, M.R.; and Klein, D.L. The mitral valve prolapse-panic disorder connection. *Psychosomatic Medicine* 50:114-122, 1988*b*.

Grant, B.; Katon, W.; and Beitman, B. Panic disorder. *Journal of Family Practice* 17:907-914, 1983.

Grant, S.J.; Huang, Y.H.; and Redmond, D.E. Benzodiazepines attenuate single unit activity in the locus coeruleus. *Life Sciences* 27:2231-2236, 1980.

Gray, J.A. Drug effects on fear and frustration: Possible limbic site of action of minor tranquilizers. In: Iverson, L.L.; Iverson, S.D.; and Snyder, S.H., eds. *Handbook of Psychopharmacology. Vol. 8: Drugs Neurotransmitters and Behavior*. New York: Plenum Press, 1977. pp. 433-529.

Gray, J.A. *The Neuropsychology of Anxiety*. Oxford: Clarendon, 1982.

Greden, J.F. Anxiety or caffeinism: A diagnostic dilemma. *American Journal of Psychiatry* 131:1089-1092, 1974.

Greenblatt, D.J., and Shader, R.I. *Benzodiazepines in Clinical Practice*. New York: Raven Press, 1974.

Grunhaus, L.; Gloger, S.; and Birmacher, B. Clomipramine treatment for panic attacks in patients with mitral valve prolapse. *Journal of Clinical Psychiatry* 45:25-27, 1984.

Guyenot, P.G., and Aghajanian, G.K. ACH, substance P and metenkephalin in the locus coeruleus: Pharmacologic evidence for independent sites of action. *European Journal of Pharmacology* 53:319-328, 1979.

Guze, S.B. *Criminality and Psychiatric Disorder*. New York: Oxford University Press, 1976.

Halaris, A. Antidepressant drug therapy in the elderly: Enhancing safety and compliance. *International Journal of Psychiatry in Medicine* 16:1-19, 1986-87.

Hamlin, C.L. "Panic Disorder, Vertigo and the Protirelin Test." Paper presented at the 140th Annual Meeting of the American Psychiatric Association, Chicago, 1987.

Hamlin, C.L., and Pottash, A.L.C. Evaluation of anxiety disorders. In: Woods, S., ed. *Diagnostic and Laboratory Testing in Psychiatry.* New York: Plenum, 1986. pp. 46-69.

Hankin, J., and Oktay, J.S. Mental disorder and primary medical care. An analytic review of the literature. In: National Institute of Mental Health, Series D, No. 7, DHEW Pub. No. (ADM)78-661, Rockville, MD: Supt. of Docs., Govt. Print. Off., 1979.

Harper, M., and Roth, M. Temporal lobe epilepsy and phobic anxiety-depersonalization syndrome. Part I: A comparative study. *Comprehensive Psychiatry* 3:129-151, 1962.

Heimberg, R.G.; Becker, R.E.; Goldfinger, K.; and Vermilyea, J.A. Treatment of social phobia by exposure, cognitive restructuring, and homework assignments. *Journal of Nervous and Mental Disease* 173:236-245, 1985.

Helzer, J.E., and Pryzbeck, T.R. The co-occurrence of alcoholism with other psychiatric disorders in the general population and its impact on treatment. *Journal of Studies on Alcohol* 49:219-224, 1988.

Heninger, G.R., and Charney, D.S. Monoamine receptor systems and anxiety disorders. *Psychiatric Clinics of North America* 11:309-326, 1988.

Hibbert, G.A. Ideational components of anxiety: Their origin and content. *British Journal of Psychiatry* 144:618-624, 1984.

Hillard, J.R., and Viewig, W.V.R. Marked sinus tachycardia resulting from the synergistic effects of marijuana and nortriptyline. *American Journal of Psychiatry* 140:626-627, 1983.

Hoeper, E.W.; Nyczi, G.R.; and Cleary, P.D. Estimated prevalence of RDC mental disorder in primary care. *International Journal of Mental Health* 8:6-15, 1979.

Hollander, E.; Liebowitz, M.R.; and Gorman, J.M. Anxiety disorders. In: Talbott, J.A.; Hales, R.E.; and Yudofsky, S.C., eds. *The American Psychiatric Press Textbook of Psychiatry.* Washington, DC: American Psychiatric Press, 1988.

Hollister, L.D. A look at the issues: Use of minor tranquilizers. *Psychosomatics* 21:4-6, 1980.

Holmberg, G., and Gershon, S. Autonomic and psychiatric effects of yohimbine hydrochloride. *Psychopharmacology* 2:93-106, 1961.

Holmgren, A., and Strom, G. Blood lactate concentrations in relation to absolute and relative work load in normal men, and in mitral stenosis, atrial septal defect and vasoregulatory asthenia. *Acta Medica Scandinavica* 103:185-193, 1959.

Hope, J.A. *A Treatise on the Disease of the Heart and Great Vessels Comprising a New View of the Physiology of the Heart's Action. According to Which the Physical Signs are Explained.* London: Churchill, 1832.

Insel, T.R.; Ninan, P.T.; Aloi, J.; Jimerson, D.; Skolnick, P.; and Paul, S.M. Bz receptors and anxiety in non-human primates. *Archives of General Psychiatry* 41:741-750, 1984.

Johnstone, E.C.; Cunningham, O.; and Frith, C.D. Neurotic illness and its response to anxiolytic and antidepressant treatment. *Psychosomatic Medicine* 10:321-328, 1980.

Jones, M. Physiological and psychological responses to stress in neurotic patients. *Journal of Mental Science* 94:392-427, 1984.

Jones, M., and Lewis, A. Effort syndrome. *Lancet* i:813-818, 1941.

Jones, M., and Mellersh, V. Comparison of exercise response in anxiety states and normal controls. *Psychosomatic Medicine* 8:180-187, 1946.

Joyce, P.R.; Bushnell, J.A.; Oakley-Browne, M.A.; Wells, J.E.; and Hornblow, A.R. The epidemiology of panic symptomatology and agoraphobic avoidance. *Comprehensive Psychiatry*, in press.

Kahn, J.F.; Drusin, R.E.; and Klein, D.F. Idiopathic cardiomyopathy and panic disorder: Clinical association in cardiac transplant candidates. *American Journal of Psychiatry* 144:1327-1330, 1987.

Kahn, R.J.; McNair, D.M.; and Lipman, L.S. Imipramine and chlordiazepoxide in depressive and anxiety disorders. II. Efficacy in anxious outpatients. *Archives of General Psychiatry* 43:79-85, 1986.

Katerndahl, D.A. The sequence of panic symptoms. *Journal of Family Practice* 26:49-52, 1988.

Katerndahl, D.A., and Vande Creek, L. Hyperthyroidism and panic attacks. *Psychosomatics* 24:491-496, 1986.

Katon, W. Panic disorder and somatization: A review of 55 cases. *American Journal of Medicine* 77:101-106, 1984.

Katon, W. Panic disorder: Epidemiology, diagnosis and treatment. *Journal of Clinical Psychiatry* 47(10):21-27, 1986.

Katon, W. The epidemiology of depression in medical care. *International Journal of Psychiatry in Medicine* 17(1):95-110, 1987.

Katon, W. Panic disorder: The importance of phenomenology. *Journal of Family Practice* 26(1):23-24, 1988.

Katon, W., and Kleinman, A.M. Doctor-patient negotiation and other social science strategies in patient care. In: Eisenberg, L., and Kleinman, A.M., eds. *The Relevance of Social Science for Medicine*. Datrecht, Holland: D. Reidel, 1980. pp. 253-259.

Katon, W., and Roy-Byrne, P.P. Antidepressants in the medically ill: Diagnosis and treatment in primary care. *Clinical Chemistry* 34:829-836, 1988.

Katon, W., and Roy-Byrne, P.P. Panic disorder in the medically ill. *Journal of Clinical Psychiatry* 50:299-302, 1989.

Katon, W., and Von Korff, M. Caseness criteria for major depression: The primary care clinician and the epidemiologist. In: Attkisson, C., and Zich, J., eds. *Screening for Depression in Primary Care*. New York: Routledge, Chapman and Hall, 1990, pp. 43-62.

Katon, W.; Ries, R.K.; and Kleinman, A. The prevalence of somatization in primary care. *Comprehensive Psychiatry* 25:208-215, 1984.

Katon, W.; Vitaliano, P.P.; Russo, J.; Jones, M.; and Anderson, K. Panic disorder: Epidemiology in primary care. *Journal of Family Practice* 23:233-239, 1986.

Katon, W.; Vitaliano, P.P.; Russo, J.; Jones, M.; and Anderson, K. Panic disorder: Spectrum of severity and somatization. *Journal of Nervous and Mental Disease* 175(1):12-19, 1987*a*.

Katon, W.; Vitaliano, P.P.; Anderson, K.; Jones, M.; and Russo, J. Panic disorder: Residual symptoms after the acute attacks abate. *Comprehensive Psychiatry* 28:151-158, 1987*b*.

Katon, W.; Hall, M.L.; Russo, J.; Cormier, L.; Hollifield, M.; Vitaliano, P.P.; and Beitman, B. Chest pain: Relationship of psychiatric illness to coronary arteriographic results. *American Journal of Medicine* 84:1-9, 1988*a*.

Katon, W.; Von Korff, M.; Lin, E.; Lipscomb, P.; Russo, J.; Polk, E.; and Wagner, E. Distressed high utilizers of medical care: DSM-III-R diagnoses and treatment needs. *Gen Hosp Psychiatry* 12:355-362, 1990.

Kemp, H.G.; Kronmal, R.A.; Vlietstra, R.E.; and Frye, R.L. Seven year survival of patients with normal or near normal coronary arteriograms: A CASS registry study. *Journal of American College of Cardiology* 7:479-483, 1986.

Klein, D.F. Delineation of two drug-responsive anxiety syndromes. *Psychopharmacology* 5:397-408, 1964.

Klein, D.F. Anxiety reconceptualized. In: Klein, D.F., and Rabkin, J., eds. *Anxiety: New Research and Changing Concepts.* New York: Raven Press, 1981.

Kleinman, A.M.; Eisenberg, L.; and Good, B. Culture, illness and care. *Annals of Internal Medicine* 88:251-258, 1978.

Kolb, L.C. The posttraumatic stress disorders of combat: A subgroup with conditioned emotional response. *Military Medicine* 149:237-243, 1984.

Kolb, L.C.; Burris, B.C.; and Griffiths, S. Propranolol and clonidine in posttraumatic stress disorders of war. In: Van der Kolk, B.A., ed. *Post-Traumatic Stress Disorder: Psychological and Biological Sequelae.* Washington, DC: American Psychiatric Press, 1984.

Kopin, I.J.; Fischer, J.E.; Musacchio, J.M.; Horst, W.D.; and Weise, V.K. "False neurochemical transmitters" and the mechanism of sympathetic blockade by monoamine oxidase inhibitors. *Journal of Pharmacology and Experimental Therapeutics* 147:186-193, 1965.

Kosten, T.R.; Mason, J.W.; Giller, E.L.; Ostross, R.; and Harkness, L. Sustained urinary norepinephrine and epinephrine elevation in posttraumatic stress disorder. *Psychoneuroendocrinology* 12:13-20, 1987.

Lader, M. Behavior and anxiety: Physiologic mechanisms. *Journal of Clinical Psychiatry* 44(11, Sect 2):5-10, 1983.

Landsberg, L., and Young, J.B. Pheochromocytoma. In: Braunwald, E.; Esselbacher, K.J.; and Petersdorf, R.G., eds. *Harrison's Principles of Internal Medicine*, 11th ed. New York: McGraw Hill, 1987.

Leckman, J.F.; Weissman, M.M.; Merikangas, K.R.; Pauls, D.L.; and Prusoff, B.A. Panic disorder and major depression. *Archives of General Psychiatry* 40:1055-1060, 1983*a*.

Leckman, J.F.; Merikangas, K.P.; Pauls, D.L.; Prusoff, B.A.; and Weissman, M.M. Anxiety disorders and depression: Contradictions between family study data and DSM-III convention. *American Journal of Psychiatry* 140:880-882, 1983*b*.

Lee, M.A.; Flegel, P.; Greden, J.F.; and Cameron, O.G. Anxiogenic effects of caffeine on panic and depressed patients. *American Journal of Psychiatry* 145:632-635, 1988.

Leff, J.P. *Psychiatry Around the Globe: A Transcultural View.* New York: Marcel Dekker, 1981.

Lesser, I.M.; Rubin, R.T.; Lydiard, R.B.; Swinson, R.; and Pecknold, J. Past and current thyroid function in subjects with panic disorder. *Journal of Clinical Psychiatry* 48:473-476, 1987.

Lewis, T. Report upon soldiers returned as cases of "Disordered Action of the Heart" (DAH) or "Valvular Disease of the Heart" (VDH). Medical Research Committee. Special Report Series, No. 8. London, 1917.

Lewis, T. *The Soldier's Heart and Effort Syndrome.* London: Shaw and Sons, 1940.

Ley, R. Agoraphobia, the panic attack and the hyperventilation syndrome. *Behaviour Research and Therapy* 23:79-81, 1985.

Liebowitz, M.R.; Fyer, A.J.; Gorman, J.; Dillon, D.; Appleby, I.; Levy, G.; Anderson, S.; Davies, S.; Palij, M.; and Klein, D.F. Lactate provocation of panic attacks: I. Clinical and behavioral findings. *Archives of General Psychiatry* 41:764-770, 1984.

Liebowitz, M.R.; Gorman, J.M.; Fyer, A.J.; Levitt, M.; Dillon, D.; Levy, G.; Appleby, I.L.; Anderson, S.; Palij, M.; Davies, S.O.; and Klein, D.F. Lactate provocation of panic attacks: II. Biochemical and physiologic findings. *Archives of General Psychiatry* 42:709-719, 1985.

Liebowitz, M.R.; Fyer, A.J.; Gorman, J.; and Klein, D.F. Recent developments in the understanding and pharmacotherapy of panic attacks. *Psychopharmacology Bulletin* 22:792-796, 1986.

Lindemann, C.G.; Zitrin, C.M.; and Klein, D.F. Thyroid dysfunction in phobic patients. *Psychosomatics* 25:603-606, 1984.

Linko, E. Lactic acid response to muscular exercise in neurocirculatory asthenia (anxiety neurosis, neurasthenia, effort syndrome). *Research Publications Association of Nervous and Mental Diseases* 29:832-869, 1950.

Linn, L.S., and Yager, J. Recognition of depression and anxiety by primary care physicians. *Psychosomatics* 25:593-600, 1984.

Liskow, B.; Othmer, E.; and Penich, E.C. Is Briquet's syndrome a heterogenous disorder? *American Journal of Psychiatry* 143:626-629, 1986.

Lum, L.C. The syndrome of habitual chronic hyperventilation. In: Hill, O.W., ed. *Modern Trends in Psychosomatic Medicine.* Vol. 3. London: Butterworth's, 1971. pp. 196-230.

Lydiard, R.B. Panic disorder: Pharmacologic treatment. *Annals of Psychiatry* 18:468-472, 1988.

Lydiard, R.B.; Laraia, M.T.; Howell, E.F.; and Ballenger, J.C. Can panic disorder present as irritable bowel syndrome? *Journal of Clinical Psychiatry* 47:470-473, 1986.

Lydiard, R.B.; Laraia, M.T.; Ballenger, J.C.; and Howell, E.F. Emergence of depressive symptoms in patients receiving alprazolam for panic disorder. *American Journal of Psychiatry* 144:664-665, 1987.

MacKenzie, J. The soldiers heart and war neurosis: A study in symptomatology. *British Medical Journal* i:491-494, 530-534, 1920.

MacKenzie, T.B., and Popkin, M.K. Organic anxiety syndrome. *American Journal of Psychiatry* 140:342-344, 1983.

Magarian, G.J. Hyperventilation syndromes: Infrequently recognized common expressions of anxiety and stress. *Medicine* 61(4):219-236, 1982.

Manger, W.M., and Gifford, R.W. Hypertension secondary to pheochromocytoma. *Bulletin of New York Academy of Medicine* 58:139-158, 1982.

Marangos, P.J.; Paul, S.M.; Parma, A.M.; Goodwin, F.K.; Synapin, P.; and Skolnick, P. Purinergic inhibition of diazepam binding to rat brain (in vitro). *Life Science* 24:851-858, 1979.

Margraf, J.; Anke, E.; and Roth, W.T. Sodium lactate infusions and panic attacks: A review and critique. *Psychosomatic Medicine* 48:23-51, 1986.

Margraf, J.; Ehlers, A.; and Roth, W.T. Panic attack associated with perceived heart rate acceleration: A case report. *Behavior Therapy* 18:84-89, 1987.

Margraf, J.; Ehlers, A.; and Roth, W.T. Mitral valve prolapse and panic disorder: A review of their relationship. *Psychosomatic Medicine* 50:93-113, 1988.

Marks, I.M. *Living With Fear.* New York: McGraw-Hill, 1978.

Marks, I.M. *Fears, Phobias and Rituals: Panic, Anxiety and Their Disorders.* New York: Oxford University Press, 1987. pp. 190-191.

Marks, I.M., and Herst, E.R. A survey of 1,200 agoraphobics in Britain. *Social Psychiatry* 5:16-24, 1970.

Marks, I.M., and Horder, J. *Phobias and Their Management,* in press.

Marks, I.M., and Tobena, A. What do the neurosciences tell us about anxiety disorders? *Psychological Medicine* 16:9-12, 1986.

Marks, J. The benzodiazepines—for good or evil. *Neuropsychobiology* 10:115-126, 1983.

Marshall, D.W.; Westmoreland, B.F.; and Sharbrough, F.W. Ictal tachycardia during temporal lobe seizures. *Mayo Clinic Proceedings* 58:443-446, 1983.

Marsland, D.W.; Wood, M.; and Mayo, F. A data bank for patient care, curriculum and research in family practice: 526,196 patient problems. *Journal of Family Practice* 3:25-68, 1976.

Martin, R.L.; Cloninger, R.; Guze, S.B.; and Clayton, P.J. Mortality in a follow-up of 500 psychiatric outpatients. *Archives of General Psychiatry* 42:47-66, 1985.

Mathew, R.J.; Ho, B.T.; Kralik, P.; Taylor, D.; Weinman, M.; Semchuk, K.; and Claghorn, J.L. Catechol-o-methyltransferase and catecholamines in anxiety and relaxation. *Psychiatry Research* 3:85-91, 1980.

Mavissakalian, M., and Hamann, M. DSM-III personality disorder in agoraphobia: II. Changes with treatment. *Comprehensive Psychiatry* 28:356-361, 1987.

McCabe, B., and Tsuang, M.T. Dietary considerations in MAO inhibitor regimens. *Journal of Clinical Psychiatry* 43:178-181, 1982.

McFarland, B.H.; Freeborn, D.K.; Mullooly, J.P.; and Pope, C.R. Utilization patterns among long-term enrollees in a prepaid group practice health maintenance organization. *Medical Care* 23:1221-1233, 1985.

Mellman, T.A., and Davis, G.C. Combat related flashbacks in posttraumatic stress disorder. Phenomenology and similarity to panic attacks. *Journal of Clinical Psychiatry* 46:379-382, 1985.

Mitchell, R.A.; Loeschke, H.H.; Severinghaus, J.W.; Richardson, B.W.; and Massion, W.H. Regions of respiratory chemosensitivity on the surface of the medulla. *Annals of the New York Academy of Sciences* 109:661-681, 1963.

Mule, S.J. The pharmacodynamics of cocaine abuse. *Psychiatric Annals* 14:724-727, 1984.

Mullaney, J.A., and Trippett, C. Alcohol dependence and phobias: Clinical description and relevance. *British Journal of Psychiatry* 135:565-573, 1979.

Myers, A.B.R. *On the Aetiology and Prevalence of Disease of the Heart Among Soldiers.* London: Churchill, 1870.

Myers, J.K.; Weissman, M.M.; Tischler, G.E.; Holzer, C.E.; Leaf, P.J.; Orvaschel, H.; Anthony, J.C.; Boyd, J.H.; Burke, J.D.; Kramer, M.; and Stoltzman, R. Six-month prevalence of psychiatric disorders in three communities. *Archives of General Psychiatry* 41:959-970, 1984.

Nesse, R.M.; Cameron, O.G.; Curtis, G.C.; McCann, D.S.; and Huber-Smith, M.J. Adrenergic function in patients with panic anxiety. *Archives of General Psychiatry* 41:771-776, 1984.

Nielson, A.C., and Williams, T.A. Depression in ambulatory medical patients. *Archives of General Psychiatry* 37:999-1004, 1980.

Nishimura, R.A.; McGoon, M.D.; Shub, C.; Miller, F.A.; Ilstrup, D.M.; and Tajik, A.J. Echocardiographically documented mitral-valve prolapse: Long-term follow-up of 237 patients. *New England Journal of Medicine* 313:1305-1309, 1985.

Norton, R.G.; Harrison, B.; Hauch, J.; and Rhodes, L. Characteristics of people with infrequent attacks. *Abnormal Psychiatry* 94:216-221, 1985.

Noyes, R., and Clancy J. Anxiety neurosis: A 5-year followup. *Journal of Nervous and Mental Disease* 162:200-205, 1976.

Noyes, R.; Clancy, J.; Crowe, R.; Hoenk, P.P.; and Slymen, D.J. The familial prevalence of anxiety neurosis. *Archives of General Psychiatry* 35:1057-1059, 1978.

Noyes, R.; Clancy, J.; Hoenk, P.R.; and Slymen, D.J. The prognosis of anxiety neurosis. *Archives of General Psychiatry* 37:173-178, 1980.

Noyes, R.; Reich, J.; Clancy, J.; and O'Gorman, T.W. Reduction in hypochondriasis with treatment of panic disorder. *British Journal of Psychiatry* 149:631-635, 1986.

Nusynowitz, M.L., and Young, R.L. Thyroid dysfunction in the ailing, aging and aberrant. *Journal of the American Medical Association* 242:275-276, 1979.

Ockene, I.S.; Shay, M.J.; Alpert, J.S.; Weiner, B.H.; and Dolen, J.E. Unexplained chest pain in patients with normal coronary arteriograms: A followup study of functional status. *New England Journal of Medicine* 303:1249-1252, 1980.

Oke, A.; Kent, T.; Preskorn, S.; and Adams, R.N. In vivo electrochemical detection of the effects of CO_2 on biogenic amine release. *Social Neuroscience Abstract* 9:1002, 1983.

Olpe, H.R.; Jones, R.S.G.; and Steinmann, M.W. The locus coeruleus: Actions of psychoactive drugs. *Experientia* 39:242-249, 1983.

Oppenheimer, B.S., and Rothschild, M.A. The psychoneurotic factor in the irritable heart of soldiers. *Journal of the American Medical Association* 70:1919-1922, 1918.

Oppenheimer, B.S.; Levine, S.A.; Morson, R.A.; Rothschild, M.A.; St. Lawrence, W.; and Wilson, F.N. Report on neurocirculatory asthenia and its management. *Military Surgeon* 42:409-426, 711-719, 1918.

Orleans, C.T.; George, L.K.; and Houpt, J.L. How primary physicians treat psychiatric disorders: A national survey of family practitioners. *Archives of General Psychiatry* 42:52-57, 1985.

Pare, C.M.B. Psychopharmacology update. *McLean Hospital Journal* 2(1):24-38, 1977.

Pare, C.M.B.; Kline, N.; Hallstrom, C.; and Cooper, T.B. Will amitriptyline prevent the "cheese" reaction of monoamine oxidase inhibitors? *Lancet* i:183-186, 1982.

Pariser, S.F.; Jones, B.A.; Pinta, E.F.; Young, E.A.; and Fontana, M.E. Panic attacks: Diagnostic evaluations of 17 patients. *American Journal of Psychiatry* 136:105-106, 1979.

Parker, G. Reported parental characteristics of agoraphobics and social phobics. *British Journal of Psychiatry* 135:555-560, 1979.

Patel, J.; Marangos, P.J.; Stivers, J.; and Goodwin, F.K. Characterization of adenosine receptors in the brain using N^6 cyclohexyl (^{3}H) adenosine. *Brain Research* 237:203-214, 1982.

Paul, S.M. Anxiety and depression: A common neurobiological substrate? *Journal of Clinical Psychiatry* 49(10 Suppl):13-16, 1988.

Pecknold, J.; Swinson, R.P.; Kuch, K.; and Lewis, C.P. Alprazolam in panic disorder and agoraphobia: Results from a multicenter trial. III. Discontinuation effects. *Archives of General Psychiatry* 45:429-436, 1988.

Perley, M.J., and Guze, S.B. Hysteria—The stability and usefulness of clinical criteria. *Diseases of the Nervous System* 33:617-621, 1962.

Petersen, R.C., and Ghoneim, M.M. Diazepam and human memory: Influence on acquisition, retrieval, and state-dependent learning. *Progress in Neuro-Psychopharmacology* 4:81-89, 1980.

Pilowsky, I., and Spence, N.D. *Manual for the Illness Behavior Questionnaire (IBQ).* 2d ed. Adelaide, South Australia: University of Adelaide, Department of Psychiatry, 1983.

Pitts, F.N., and McClure, J.N. Lactate metabolism in anxiety neurosis. *New England Journal of Medicine* 277:1329-1336, 1967.

Poice, J.L., and Marall, D.G. An autoradiographic study of the projections of the central nucleus of the monkey amygdala. *Journal of Neurosurgical Sciences* 1:1242-1259, 1981.

Post, R.M.; Uhde, T.W.; and Putnam, F.W. Kindling and carbamazine in affective illness. *Journal of Nervous and Mental Disease* 170:717-731, 1984.

Quitkin, F.M.; Rifkin, A.; Kaplan, J.; and Klein, D.F. Phobic anxiety syndrome complicated by drug dependence and addiction. A treatable form of drug abuse. *Archives of General Psychiatry* 27:159-162, 1972.

Rainey, J.M., Jr.; Ettedgui, E.; and Pohl, R.B. The beta-receptor: Isoproterenol anxiety states. *Psychopathology* 17(Suppl 3):40-51, 1984a.

Rainey, J.M.; Pohl, R.B.; Williams, M.; Knitter, E.; Freedman, R.R.; and Ettedgui, E. A comparison of lactate and isoproteranol anxiety states. *Psychopathology* 17(3):74-82, 1984b.

Rainey, J.M.; Frohman, C.E.; Warner, K.; Bates, S.; Pohl, R.B.; and Yeragani, V. Panic anxiety and lactate metabolism. *Psychopharmacology Bulletin* 21:434-437, 1985.

Rainey, J.M.; Aleem, A.; Ortiz, A.; Yeragani, V.; Pohl, R.; and Berchou, R. A laboratory procedure for the induction of flashbacks. *Archives of General Psychiatry* 144:1317-1323, 1987.

Raj, A., and Sheehan, D.V. Medical evaluation of panic attacks. *Journal of Clinical Psychiatry* 48:309-313, 1987.

Rapee, R.M., and Barlow, D.H. Panic disorder: Cognitive-behavioral treatment. *Psychiatric Annals* 18:473-477, 1988.

Raskin, A.; Schulterbrandt, J.G.; Reating, N.; Crook, T.H.; and Odle, D. Depression subtypes in response to phenelzine, diazepam, and a placebo:

Results of a nine hospital collaborative study. *Archives of General Psychiatry* 30:66-75, 1974.

Raskin, M.; Peeke, H.V.S.; Dickman, W.; and Pinsker, H. Panic and generalized anxiety disorders: Developmental antecedents and precipitants. *Archives of General Psychiatry* 39:687-689, 1982.

Redmond, D.E. New and old evidence for the involvement of a brain norepinephrine system in anxiety. In: Fann, W.E.; Karacan, J.; Pokoiny, A.D.; and Williams, R.L., eds. *The Phenomenology and Treatment of Anxiety.* New York: Spectrum, 1979. pp. 153-203.

Redmond, D.E.; Huang, Y.M.; Snyder, D.R.; and Maas, J.W. Behavioral effects of stimulation of the nucleus coeruleus in the stump-tailed monkey macaca arctoides. *Brain Research* 116:502-510, 1976.

Regier, D.A.; Boyd, J.H.; Burke J.D., Rae, D.S.; Myers, J.K.; Kramer, M.; Robins, L.N.; George, L.K.; Karno, M.; Locke, B.Z. One-month prevalence of mental disorders in the United States: Based on five epidemiologic catchment area sites. *Archives of General Psychiatry* 45:977-986, 1988.

Regier, D.; Goldberg, I.D.; and Taube, C.H. The de facto U.S. mental health service system. *Archives of General Psychiatry* 35:685-693, 1978.

Reich, J. The epidemiology of anxiety. *Journal of Nervous and Mental Disease* 174:129-136, 1986.

Reich, J., and Troughton, E. Comparison of DSM-III personality disorders in recovered depressed and panic disorder patients. *Journal of Nervous and Mental Disease* 176:300-304, 1988.

Reiman, E.M.; Raichle, M.E.; Robins, E.; Butler, F.K.; Herscovitch, P.; Fox, P.; and Perlmutter, J. The application of positron emission tomography to the study of panic disorder. *American Journal of Psychiatry* 143:469-477, 1986.

Roberts, A.H. Housebound wives: A follow-up study of a phobic-anxiety state. *British Journal of Psychiatry* 110:191-197, 1964.

Roberts, R. An integrated approach to the treatment of panic disorder. *American Journal of Psychotherapy* 38:413-430, 1984.

Robins, L.N.; Helzer, J.E.; Groughan, J.; and Ratcliff, K.S. National Institute of Mental Health Diagnostic Interview Schedule: Its history, characteristics and validity. *Archives of General Psychiatry* 38:381-389, 1981.

Robins, L.N.; Helzer, J.E.; Weissman, M.M.; Orvaschel, H.; Gruenberg, E.; Burke, J.D.; and Regier, D.A. Lifetime prevalence of specific psychiatric disorders in three sites. *Archives of General Psychiatry* 41:949-958, 1984.

Robinson, J.O., and Granfield, A.J. The frequent consulter in primary medical care. *Journal of Psychosomatic Research* 30:589-600, 1986.

Roose, S.P.; Glassman, A.H.; Giardina, E.G.V.; Johnson, L.L.; Walsh, B.T.; Woodring, S.; and Bigger, J.T., Jr. Nortriptyline in depressed patients with left ventricular impairment. *Journal of American Medical Association* 256:3253-3257, 1986.

Rosen, G.; Kleinman, A.; and Katon, W. Somatization in family practice: A biopsychosocial approach. *Journal of Family Practice* 14:493-502, 1982.

Rosenbaum, J.F. The drug treatment of anxiety. *New England Journal of Medicine* 7:401-403, 1982.

Rosenbaum, J.; Biederman, J.; Gershen, M.; Hirschfeld, D.R.; Meminger, S.R.; Herman, J.B.; Kagan, J.; Resnick, J.S.; and Snidman, N. Behavioral inhibition in children of parents with panic disorder and agoraphobia. *Archives of General Psychiatry* 45:463-470, 1988.

Rosenthal, M.E.; Hamer, A.; Gang, E.S.; Oseran, D.S.; Mandel, W.J.; and Peter, T. The yield of programmed ventricular stimulation of mitral valve prolapse patients with ventricular arrhythmias. *American Heart Journal* 110:970-976, 1985.

Roth, M. The phobic-anxiety depersonalization syndrome. *Proceedings of Royal Society of Medicine* 52:587-595, 1959.

Roth, M. The phobic anxiety-depersonalization syndrome and some general aetiological problems in psychiatry. *Journal of Neuropsychiatry* 1:293-306, 1960.

Roth, W.T.; Telch, M.J.; Taylor, C.B.; Sachitaro, J.A.; Gallen, C.C.; Kopell, M.L.; McClenahan, K.L.; Agras, W.S.; and Pfefferbaum, A. Autonomic characteristics of agoraphobia with panic attacks. *Biological Psychiatry* 21:1133-1154, 1985.

Roy-Byrne, P.P., and Cowley, D. Panic disorder: Biological aspects. *Psychiatric Annals* 18:457-463, 1988.

Roy-Byrne, P.P., and Katon, W. An update on treatment of the anxiety disorders. *Hospital and Community Psychiatry* 38:835-843, 1987.

Roy-Byrne, P.P., and Uhde, T.W. Exogenous factors in panic disorder: Clinical and research implications. *Journal of Clinical Psychiatry* 49:56-60, 1988.

Roy-Byrne, P.P.; Geraci, M.; and Uhde, T. Life events and the onset of panic disorder. *American Journal of Psychiatry* 143:1424-1427, 1986.

Roy-Byrne, P.P.; Uhde, T.W.; Rubinow, D.R.; and Post, R.M. Reduced TSH and prolactin responses to TRH in patients with panic disorder. *American Journal of Psychiatry* 143:503-507, 1986.

Roy-Byrne, P.P.; Mellman, T.A.; and Uhde, T.W. Biologic findings in panic disorder. *Journal of Anxiety Disorders* 2:17-29, 1988.

Roy-Byrne, P.P.; Cowley, D.S.; and Katon, W. Pharmacotherapy of anxiety disorders. In: *Textbook of Therapeutic Medicine for Practicing Physicians*, in press.

Salkovskis, P.M.; Jones, D.R.O.; and Clark, D.M. Respiratory control in the treatment of panic attacks: Replication and extension with concurrent measurement of behavior and pCO_2. *British Journal of Psychiatry* 148:526-532, 1986.

Sanderson, W.C.; Rapee, R.M.; and Barlow, D.H. The influence of an illusion of control on panic attacks induced via inhalation of 5.5% carbon dioxide-enriched air. *Archives of General Psychiatry* 46:157-162, 1989.

Sarason, I.G. Theories of anxiety and its clinical treatment. *Journal of Drug Research* 7:7-15, 1982.

Sargant, W. The treatment of anxiety states and atypical depressions by the monoamine oxidase inhibitor drugs. *Journal of Neuropsychiatry* 1(3):96-103, 1962.

Schachter, S., and Singer, J.E. Cognitive, social and physiologic determinants of emotional state. *Psychological Review* 69:379-399, 1962.

Schildkraut, J.J. The catecholamine hypothesis of affective disorders: A review of supporting evidence. *American Journal of Psychiatry* 122:509-522, 1965.

Schulberg, H.C.; Saul, M.; and McClelland, M. Assessing depression in primary medical and psychiatric pactices. *Archives of General Psychiatry* 12:1164-1170, 1985.

Schurman, R.A.; Kramer, P.D.; and Mitchel, J.B. The hidden mental health network: Treatment of mental illness by nonpsychiatrist physicians. *Archives of General Psychiatry* 42:89-94, 1985.

Segal, M. Serotonergic innervation of the locus coeruleus from the dorsal raphe and its action on responses to noxious stimuli. *Journal of Physiology* 286:401-415, 1979.

Shapiro, S.; Skinner, E.A.; Kessler, L.G.; Von Korff, M.; German, P.S.; Tischler, G.L.; Leaf, P.J.; Benham, L.; Cottler, L.; and Regier, D.A. Utilization of health and mental health services: Three epidemiologic catchment area sites. *Archives of General Psychiatry* 41:971-978, 1984.

Shear, M.K. Pathophysiology of panic: A review of pharmacologic provocative tests and naturalistic monitoring data. *Journal of Clinical Psychiatry* 47(6):18-26, 1986.

Shear, M.K.; Kligfield, P.; Harshfield, G.; Devereux, R.B.; Polan, J.J.; Mann, J.J.; Pickering, T.; and Frances, A.J. Cardiac rate and rhythm in panic patients. *American Journal of Psychiatry* 144:633-637, 1987.

Sheehan, D.V. Panic attacks and phobias. *New England Journal of Medicine* 307:156-158, 1982.

Sheehan, D.V. *The Anxiety Disease.* New York: Scribner, 1983.

Sheehan, D.V. Delineation of anxiety and phobic disorders responsive to monoamine oxidase inhibitors: Implications for classification. *Journal of Clinical Psychiatry* 45(7, Sec. 2):29-36, 1984.

Sheehan, D.V., and Sheehan, K.H. The classification of anxiety and hysterical states. I. Historical review and empirical delineation. *Journal of Clinical Psychopharmacology* 1:235-244, 1982.

Sheehan, D.V.; Ballenger, J.; and Jacobsen, G. Treatment of endogenous anxiety with phobic, hysterical and hypochondriacal symptoms. *Archives of General Psychiatry* 37:51-59, 1980.

Sheehan, D.V.; Sheehan, K.F.; and Minichiello, W.E. Age of onset of phobic disorders: A reevaluation. *Comprehensive Psychiatry* 22:544-553, 1981.

Sheehan, D.V.; Claycomb, J.B.; and Surman, O.S. "Comparison of Phenelzine, Imipramine, Alprazolam and Placebo in the Treatment of Panic Attacks and Agoraphobia." Paper presented at the American Psychiatric Association Annual Meeting, Los Angeles, 1984.

Silove, D. Perceived parental characteristics and reports of early parental deprivation in agoraphobic patients. *Australian and New Zealand Journal of Psychiatry* 20:365-369, 1986.

Skerrit, P.W. Anxiety and the heart—A historical review. *Psychological Medicine* 13:17-25, 1983.

Skolnick, P., and Paul, S.M. New concepts in the neurobiology of anxiety. *Journal of Clinical Psychiatry* 44:12-19, 1983.

Smail, P.; Stockwell, T.; Canter, S.; and Hodgson, R. Alcohol dependence and phobic anxiety states. I. A prevalence study. *British Journal of Psychiatry* 144:53-57, 1984.

Snyder, D.R.; Huang, Y.H.; and Redmond, D.E. Contribution of the locus ceruleus-noradrenergic system to cardioacceleration in nonhuman primates. *Social Neuroscience Abstract* 828, 1977.

Snyder, S.H., and Sklar, P. Behavior and molecular actions of caffeine: Focus on adenosine. *Journal of Psychiatry Research* 18:91-106, 1984.

Soley, M.H., and Schock, N.W. The etiology of the effort syndrome. *American Journal of Science* 196:840-851, 1938.

Solyom, L.; Silberfeld, M.; and Solyom, C. Maternal overprotection in the etiology of agoraphobia. *Canadian Psychiatric Association Journal* 21:109-113, 1976.

Spielberger, C.D.; Lushene, R.E.; and McAdoo, W.G. Theory and measurement of anxiety states. In: Cattel, R.B., ed. *Handbook of Modern Personality Theory*. Chicago: Aldine, 1971.

Stanburg, S.W., and Thompson, A.E. The renal response to respiratory alkalosis. *Clinical Science* 11:357-374, 1952.

Starkman, M.N.; Zelnik, T.C.; Nesse, R.M.; and Cameron, O.G. Anxiety in patients with pheochromocytoma. *Archives of Internal Medicine* 145:248-252, 1985.

Stein, M.B., and Uhde, T.W. Thyroid indices in panic disorder. *American Journal of Psychiatry* 145:745-747, 1988.

Stockwell, T.; Smail, S.; Hodgson, R.; and Carter, S. Alcohol dependence and phobic anxiety states: II. A retrospective study. *British Journal of Psychiatry* 144:58-63, 1984.

Stoeckle, J.D.; Zola, I.K.; and Davidson, G.D. The quantity and significance of psychological distress in medical patients. *Journal of Chronic Diseases* 17:959-970, 1964.

Stone, E.A. Problems with current catecholamine hypothesis of antidepressant agents: Speculations leading to a new hypothesis. *Behavior Brain Sciences* 6:535-577, 1983.

Stone, T.W. Physiologic roles for adenosine and adenosine 5'-triphosphate in the nervous system. *Neuroscience* 6:523-555, 1981.

Suomi, S.J. Ethology: Animal models of psychopathology. In: Sadock, B., ed. *Comprehensive Textbook of Psychiatry.* Baltimore: Williams & Wilkins, 1984.

Svensson, T.H. Peripheral, autonomic regulation of locus coeruleus noradrenergic neurons in brain: Putative implications for psychiatry and psychopharmacology. *Psychopharmacology* 92:1-7, 1987.

Svensson, T.H., and Usdin, T. Feedback inhibition of brain noradrenalin neurons by tricyclic antidepressants: Alpha-receptor mediation. *Science* 202:1089-1091, 1978.

Taylor, C.B.; Agras, W.S.; Roth, W.T.; King, R.; Dorian, B.; and Sheikh, J. "Ambulatory Heart Rate Changes in Panic Patients." Paper presented at the 138th Meeting of the American Psychiatric Association, Dallas, 1985.

Tesar, G.E.; Rosenbaum, J.F.; Biederman, J.; Weilburg, J.B.; Pollack, M.H.; Gross, C.C.; Falk, W.E.; Gastfriend, D.R.; Zusky, P.M.; and Bouckoms, A. Orthostatic hypotension and antidepressant pharmacotherapy. *Psychopharmacology Bulletin* 23:182-186, 1987*a*.

Tesar, G.E.; Rosenbaum, J.F.; Pollack, M.H.; Herman, J.B.; Sachs, G.S.; Mahoney, E.M.; Cohen, L.S.; McNamara, M.; and Goldstein, S. Clonazepam versus alprazolam in the treatment of panic disorder: Interim analyses of data from a prospective, double blind, placebo-controlled trial. *Journal of Clinical Psychiatry* 48(Oct. suppl):16-19, 1987*b*.

Thompson, J.W.; Burns, B.J.; Barkto, J.; Boyd, J.H.; Taube, C.A.; and Bourdon, K.H. The use of ambulatory services by persons with and without phobia. *Medical Care* 26:183-198, 1988.

Tollefson, G.D. Monoamine oxidase inhibitors: A review. *Journal of Clinical Psychiatry* 44:280-288, 1983.

Torgerson, S. Genetic factors in anxiety disorders. *Archives of General Psychiatry* 40:1085-1092, 1983.

Tucker, W.I. Diagnosis and treatment of the phobic reaction. *American Journal of Psychiatry* 112:825-830, 1956.

Turner, T.H. Agoraphobia and hyperthyroidism. *British Journal of Psychiatry* 145:215-216, 1984.

Tyrer, P.J.; Casey, P.; and Gall, J. Relationship between neurosis and personality disorder. *British Journal of Psychiatry* 142:404-408, 1983.

Uhde, T.W., and Tancer, M.E. Chemical models of panic: A review and critique. In: Tyrer, P., ed. *Psychopharmacology of Anxiety.* Oxford: University Press, 1988.

Uhde, T.W.; Vittone, B.J.; and Post, R.M. Glucose tolerance testing in panic disorder. *American Journal of Psychiatry* 141:1461-1463, 1984.

Uhde, T.W.; Boulenger, J.; Roy-Byrne, P.P.; Vittone, B.J.; Geraci, M.; and Post, R.M. Longitudinal course of panic disorder: Clinical and biological considerations. *Progress in Neuropsychopharmacology and Biological Psychiatry* 9:39-51, 1985a.

Uhde, T.W.; Roy-Byrne, P.P.; Vittone, B.J.; Boulenger, J.P.; and Post, R.M. Phenomenology and neurobiology of panic disorder. In: Maser, J.D., and Tuma, A.H., eds. *Anxiety and Anxiety Disorders.* Englewood Cliffs, NJ: Erlbaum, 1985b. pp. 557-579.

Uhlenhuth, E.H.; Bolter, M.D.; Mellinger, G.D.; Cisin, I.H.; and Clinthorne, J. Symptom checklist syndromes in the general population: Corrections with psychotherapeutic drug use. *Archives of General Psychiatry* 40:1167-1173, 1983.

Valbona, C. *Monthly Statistical Report.* Casa de Amigo Community Health Clinic. Texas, 1973.

Van Vliet, P.D.; Burchell, H.B.; and Titus, J.L. Focal myocarditis associated with pheochromocytoma. *New England Journal of Medicine* 274:1102-1108, 1966.

Veith, R.C.; Raskind, M.A.; Caldwell, J.H.; Barnes, R.G.; Gumbreght, G.M.; and Ritchie, J.L. Cardiovascular effects of tricyclic antidepressants in depressed patients with chronic heart disease. *New England Journal of Medicine* 306:954-959, 1982.

Villacres, E.C.; Hollifield, M.; Katon, W.; Wilkinson, C.; and Veith, R.C. Sympathetic nervous system activity in panic disorder. *Psychiatry Research* 21:313-321, 1987.

Vitaliano, P.P.; Russo, J.; Carr, J.E. The Ways of Coping Checklist: Psychometric properties. *Multivariate Behaviorial Research* 20:3-26, 1985.

Vitaliano, P.P.; Katon, W.; Russo, J.; Maiuro, R.D.; Anderson, K.; and Jones, M. Coping as an index of illness behavior in panic disorder. *Journal of Nervous and Mental Disease* 175(2):78-84, 1987.

Von Korff, M.; Shapiro, S.; Burke, J.D.; Teitelbaum, M.; Skinner, E.A.; German, P.; Turner, R.W.; Klein, L.; Burns, B. Anxiety and depression in a primary care clinic: Comparison of Diagnostic Interview Schedule, General Health Questionnaire, and practitioner assessments. *Archives of General Psychiatry* 44:152-156, 1987.

Walker, E.; Katon, W.; Harrop-Griffiths, J.; Holm, L.; Russo, J.; Hickok, L.R. Relationship of chronic pelvic pain to psychiatric diagnoses and childhood sexual abuse. *American Journal of Psychiatry* 145:75-80, 1988.

Wall, M.; Tuckman, M.; and Mielke, D. Panic attacks and temporal lobe seizures associated with right temporal lobe arteriovenous malformations: Case report. *Journal of Clinical Psychiatry* 46:143-145, 1985.

Wall, M.; Mielke, D.; and Luther, J.S. Panic attacks and psychomotor seizures following right temporal lobectomy. *Journal of Clinical Psychiatry* 47:219, 1986.

Warth, D.C.; King, M.E.; Cohen, J.M.; Tesumero, V.L.; March, E.: and Weyman, A.E. Prevalence of mitral valve prolapse in normal children. *Journal of American College of Cardiology* 5:1173-1177, 1985.

Weder, A.B., and Julius, S. Behavior, blood pressure variability and hypertension. *Psychosomatic Medicine* 47:406-414, 1985.

Weekes, C. *Simple, Effective Treatment of Agoraphobia.* New York: Bantam Books, 1976.

Weiss, B., and Laties, V. Enhancement of human performance by caffeine and the amphetamines. *Pharmacological Reviews* 14:1-36, 1962.

Weissman, M.M.; Myers, J.K.; and Harding, P.S. Psychiatric disorders in a U.S. urban community: 1975-1976. *American Journal of Psychiatry* 135:459-462, 1978.

Weissman, M.M.; Leckman, J.F.; Merikangas, K.R.; Gammon, G.D.; and Prusoff, B.A. Depression and anxiety disorders in parents and children. *Archives of General Psychiatry* 41:845-852, 1984.

Weissman, N.J.; Shear, M.K.; Kramer-Fox, R.; and Devereux, R.B. Contrasting patterns of autonomic dysfunction in patients with mitral valve prolapse and panic attacks. *American Journal of Medicine* 82:880-888, 1987.

Wells, K.B.; Goldberg, G.; Brook, R.H.; and Leake, B. Quality of care for psychotropic drug use in internal medicine group practices. *Western Journal of Medicine* 145:710-714, 1986.

Wernicke, J.F. The side effect profile and safety of fluoxetine. *Journal of Clinical Psychiatry* 46:(3 Sec.2):59-67, 1985.

Wheeler, E.O.; White, P.D.; and Reed, E.W. Neurocirculatory asthenia: A twenty year follow-up of one hundred and seventy-three patients. *Journal of the American Medical Association* 142:878-889, 1950.

Williams, J.C. *Practical Observations on Nervous and Sympathetic Palpitations of the Heart, as Well as on Palpitation, the Result of Organic Disease.* London: Churchill, 1836.

Winokur, G., and Black, D.W. Psychiatric and medical diagnoses as risk factors for mortality in psychiatric patients. A case-control study. *American Journal of Psychiatry* 144:208-211, 1987.

Woerner, P.I., and Guze, S.B. A family and marital study of hysteria. *British Journal of Psychiatry* 114:161-168, 1968.

Wolf, S. Sustained contraction of the diaphragm, the mechanism of a common type of dyspnea and precordial pain. *Journal of Clinical Investigation* 26:1201, 1947.

Wood, P. Aetiology of DaCosta's syndrome. *British Journal of Psychiatry* 1:845-851, 1941.

Wood, P.W. DaCosta's syndrome (or effort syndrome). *British Medical Journal* i:767-772, 805-811, 845-851, 1941.

Woods, S.W.; Charney, D.S.; Heninger, G.R.; Goodman, W.K.; Coke, J.; Redmond, D.E. Mechanisms of CO_2-induced anxiety. *Social Neuroscience Abstract* 11:132, 1985.

Woods, S.W.; Charney, D.S.; and Silver, J.M. "Benzodiazepine Receptor Antagonist Effects in Panic Disorder." Paper presented at the 141st Annual Meeting of the American Psychiatric Association, Montreal, 1988a.

Woods, S.W.; Charney, D.S.; Goodman, W.K.; and Heninger, G.R. Carbon dioxide-induced anxiety. *Archives of General Psychiatry* 45:43-52, 1988b.

Wyatt, R.J.; Portnoy, B.; Kupfer, D.J.; Snyder, F.; and Engelman, K. Resting plasma catecholamine concentrations in patients with depression and anxiety. *Archives of General Psychiatry* 24:65-70, 1971.

Wynne, J. Mitral valve prolapse. *New England Journal of Medicine* 314:577-578, 1986.

Yager, J., and Young, R.T. Non-hypoglycemia is an epidemic condition. *New England Journal of Medicine* 291:907-908, 1974.

Yeragani, V.K.; Rainey, J.M.; Pohl, R.; Ortiz, A.; Weinberg, R.N.; and Gershon, S. Thyroid hormone levels in panic disorder. *Canadian Journal of Psychiatry* 32:467-469, 1987.

Young, S.J.; Alpers, D.H.; Norland, C.C.; and Woodruff, R.A. Psychiatric illness and the irritable bowel syndrome. Practical implications for the primary physician. *Gastroenterology* 70:162-166, 1976.

Zitrin, C.M.; Klein, D.F.; Woerner, M.G.; and Ross, D.C. Treatment of phobias. I. Comparison of imipramine and placebo. *Archives of General Psychiatry* 40:125-138, 1983.

Zoccolillo, M., and Cloninger, C.R. Somatization disorder: Psychological symptoms, social disability and diagnosis. *Comprehensive Psychiatry* 27:65-73, 1986.

Zung, W.W.K. Assessment of anxiety disorder: Qualitative and quantitative approaches. In: Fann, W.E.; Karacan, I.; Pokorny, A.D.; and Williams, R.L., eds. *Phenomenology and Treatment of Anxiety*. New York: Spectrum, 1979. pp. 1-17.

Zung, W.W.K. Prevalence of clinically significant anxiety in a family practice setting. *American Journal of Psychiatry* 1471-1472, 1986.

Index